1 By the rivers of Babylon, there we sat down, yea, we wept, when we remembered Zion.

2 We hanged our harps upon the willows in the midst thereof.

3 For there they that carried us away captive required of us a song; and they that wasted us required of us mirth, saying, Sing us one of the songs of Zion.

4 How shall we sing The LORD'S song in a *strange* land?
Psalms 137:1-4

The LORD's Song

In A *Strange* Land

Billy Oatman

This is a work of fiction. All Names, characters, businesses, places, events, and incidents are either the products of the author's imagination or used in a fictional manner. Any resemblance to actual person, living or dead, or actual events is purely coincidental.

Table of Contents

Acknowledgements

First, I would like to acknowledge my Lord and Savior Jesus Christ. Secondly, I would like to make mention of my beloved parents, Elder William Oatman, Jr., and Mother Avada Oatman. My parents bought me up without smothering me with dogmatic religious restrictions. They allowed me to find Jesus for myself. They shaped my entire religious experience.

Admittedly, I am not a great musician; in fact, I can barely read music, and struggle a great deal playing by ear. This fictional book, however, would like to acknowledge the gifted and talented musicians, singers, and worship leaders who utilized Gospel music to encourage people, and uplift true and sincere praises to the Lord.

My friend, Anthony Charles Harris displayed the qualities of a dedicated musician of the Gospel, and was an example of sincere sacrifice. He has gone one to be with the Lord and is truly missed by all who knew him.

The writer would like to acknowledge the help and cooperation from Nora Lee and William Oatman, V, who aided in editing this book. I would also like to thank one of my students from my Autistic Support Class, Robbie Epps for his artwork. I would like to extend my appreciation to Kevin Harris, who is not only among my best friends, but he is also a gifted, sincere, and anointed minister of music. Finally, I would like to acknowledge my niece, Natalie Oatman. She has been an inspiration through her dedicated and Spirit-filled ministry of singing praises unto the LORD. She is truly one of *Yahweh's True Psalmist.* **William (Billy) Oatman, III**

Preface

The *Conned Vocation* was the writer's first attempt to write a novel regarding a fictional church, Movement of Our Lord Anointed Leaders (MOOLAH). *The Conned Vocation*, though filled with poetry and humor, was actually examining the political and worldly aspects of some, if not, of too many churches.

The Lord's Song in a Strange Land is a continuation of the *Conned Vocation Series* and includes some of the main characters from the original *Conned Vocation*. However, this novel examines the world of a fictional international Gospel music organization. This organization holds an annual assembly every year in a different location within the United States.

Our protagonist Timothy Samuels is assigned to cover this year's convention which is being held in Cincinnati, Ohio. Timothy faces new challenges that forces him to question everything in his life. He ponders whether or not he should remain a part of Karen, his significant other's life. He also doubts whether or not he can properly provide for his daughter, Teresa. He is thoroughly confused about the sincerity of the most popular and influential Gospel artists. He again questions the existence of God as he struggles to overcome a mounting drug addiction.

Timothy must also unravel the ongoing strange events happening to the Gospel artists who are attending the Gospel Performers Organization of the World (G-POW) Annual Convention.

Though this book is fiction, it takes an honest look at the sincerity of the performers of God's music. Are we magnifying ourselves, or are we heaping praise on ourselves? The sole purpose of Gospel Music should be the worship and praise of our Lord and Savior, Jesus Christ, and uplifting our fellow man.

William (Billy) Oatman, III

Chapter 1

"Taking Shots"

"That they may shoot in secret at the perfect: suddenly do they shoot at him, and fear not." PSALM 64:4

The sleek Mercedes-Benz S-class Maybach glided up the winding driveway as Zachariah Phillips pressed the home-link button and opened one of the three doors of his immense garage. He paused, lit a Marlboro Menthol cigarette, and glanced over at his adopted son, Amoz Phillips. Zachariah cracked the door as the dome light gradually illuminated the car.

"Well," Amoz managed to utter. "You've got to smoke another one of those cancer-sticks, and besides, what are we waiting for? I'm tired. It seemed like we were in church forever."

Zachariah's gravelly voice grunted, "It wasn't that long, son. I thought service went rather quickly tonight. You have a habit of exaggerating." He coughed a few times and then glanced over at his son.

Amoz opened the passenger door, sucked his teeth to show his disgust, and headed toward the door which led from the garage to the kitchen. "You've really been coughing a lot lately. It's those cigarettes. I'm tired, I'll catch you later, Dad."

"Wait, son. I'm coming." Zachariah said as he eased from behind the walnut wrapped steering wheel.

Amoz halted, looked over toward Zachariah and uttered, "You don't have to hurry on account of me. I can find my way by myself."

Zachariah lumbered toward Amoz and in a piercingly agitated voice blurted, "You know boy, I'm about sick and tired of your sass. I mean look at all I've done for you. You're so ungrateful."
As both men entered the kitchen almost simultaneously, Amoz grunted, "You've done for me? You've done for me? What in God's name have you ever done for me?"

Zachariah's breathing increased as he gasped for air and continued to puff on his cigarette. "Boy, you…you." He managed to catch a little more breath. "I raised you better than for you to use God's name in vain." He then began to struggle again for much needed air.

Amoz showed no hint of sympathy as his father struggled to breathe. "Here you are gagging for air as you continue to smoke and preach about living a holy life. You're the one that's ungrateful. Your tired butt should have been dead years ago. Maybe that's why God is punishing you."

"How in the world is God punishing me?" Zachariah interjected. "I'm highly favored by God. I have a blossoming and ever-growing church. I am known as the Emperor of Music in the Gospel industry. I have more Grammys and more Dove awards than any other Gospel recording artist. Last year I created the score for a hit movie. I've won more BET awards than any other artists in the Gospel music industry."

The two continued the heated discussion as they entered into the family room. "Look Dad, I know you have all that. You also have your own Gospel satellite radio station and your own record label. You're on television all the time. You're pastoring a large, or shall I dare say*: mega church*? You're a successful author. I know all that. All this material stuff doesn't make you favored or blessed." Amoz headed toward the winding stairs toward his bedroom. "I'm tired, Dad. I'm going to bed."

Zachariah lowered the volume of his voice to ease the tension. "Okay. Okay. What's the real cause of all this drama? Maybe I should increase your allowance. Or perhaps I could trade your Infiniti in for that new car that you've been bugging me about."

Amoz stopped midway on the stairs. "Jesus, Dad you just don't get it, do you? A few days ago, someone shot up your car. That should have been a wake-up call."

Zachariah chuckled. "Man, are you kidding? I was driving through the 'hood. There's always shooting and what not in the hood. That was probably some Blood or Crip thing. You don't have to worry about that again. Now I have bullet proof glass and run-flat tires on the 'Benz."

Amoz turned completely around and headed back down the stairs toward his father. "Dad, have you forgotten the letters that we've been receiving for the last couple weeks? You know, the letters and e-mails that threatened us and the other major Gospel artists? Do you remember the Scripture he included with his last letter?"

Zachariah chuckled again. "Is that what's bugging you? Some anonymous fool writes a stupid letter and you're all bent out of shape? Some clown who calls himself 'Yahweh's True Psalmist' has gotten you afraid like some little punk?"

Amoz pointed out, "Dad, it's more than that. This Yah man or woman, or whatever, quoted some crazy scripture from the book of Psalms. The Book of praise in the Bible. Remember what he wrote: *'They that shoot in secret at the blameless.'* Think about it, Dad. Can you truthfully say that we are *'blameless'*? Are we *'perfect'* as the Scripture said? This is just no coincidence that we were shot at. Those gun shots might just be a warning. Besides, it's this whole situation that we've been in for years that may be coming to a head. Now, don't get me wrong. I appreciate everything you've done for me ever since you took me in and adopted me as your son. At first, I was so proud to be a part of your

4

choir. You said that I was a child protégé. Man, I was so proud. I was a male soprano, and I didn't have to use a falsetto voice. That was my natural voice. "

The tension between the two seemed somehow to cool down. Zachariah then pointed out, "Yeah, you had a right to be proud. God gave you a special talent. Your countertenor voice was heard on some of my best-selling recordings. Your vocal lead on my updated version of *Throw Out the Lifeline* was the top selling traditional Gospel song last year."

"Yeah," Amoz interjected. "But there's more to life than hit records, Dad, and you, of all people, should know what I mean. Come on, Dad, you know--"

Zachariah interrupted, "Hey, okay, let's deal with it tomorrow. We're both tired."

"No Dad," Amoz insisted. "Let's deal with it now."

"I'll tell you what son, why don't we just table this for now? I'm not feeling too well. If it will make you feel a little more secure. I can get Timothy Samuels, the blogger-photographer to cover and investigate the upcoming Gospel Convention. We'll pay him to find out how many other artists have received any threats from this Yahweh's True Psalmist. Timothy can publish this mess on his blog and get feed-back from the other artists that might lead us to finding out who this Yahweh's True Psalmist is. And in addition to that, I will hire a bodyguard on a 24-hour 7 day a week basis. I will also boost up our security and alarm system."

Amoz pondered his father's suggestions, and then he added, "That's all cool, but this Yahweh's True Psalmist is dealing more than just bodily threats – I think he's all about a spiritual warfare. Besides that, Dad, I wouldn't involve this Timothy Samuels. He kind of wavers in his belief in God. He likes to dig and dig until he finds what he concludes may be the right answers. Sometimes his conclusions are way off and based on his bias opinions about the Body of Christ. Do you really want him to delve into *our* past, and especially yours?"

Zachariah walked over to his son, placed his arms on his shoulder, kissed him gently on his cheek, and said, "I don't have anything to hide."

Amoz wiped the moisture off his face and said, "Really? Nothing to hide. You know that there happened to be rumors about us. When I first began to sing in your choir, the rumors began. The gossip spread because you never got married, or even considered having a wife. In fact, you've never even been associated with a woman."

"Now son," Zachariah maintained. "You know that my ministry doesn't allow time for me to deal with a wife or a family. In fact, you and I are the only family we need."

6

"Yeah," Amoz smirked. "But the Bible says that it's better to marry than to burn."

"Yeah. Yeah. Yeah. We all know that, but Jesus never got married either."

"Right, Dad," Amoz mumbled as he gazed directly into his father's weary eyes. "But Jesus never seduced his disciples; and if he had a son, I'm sure he wouldn't have seduced him either."

Zachariah stormed up the stairs, rushing past his son and raised his voice slightly, "You had to bring that up again! You're just so ungrateful for all I've done for you."

Amoz slowly dragged himself up to the top of the stairs and entered his bedroom. "You surely gave me a lot of things. Just remember this: what you took away from me superseded what you could ever have given me. You took away my innocence, and my manhood. You even took away my virginity. Good night, Zack"

The sound of his son referring to him as 'Zack', cut him severely and was unbearable for Zachariah Phillips. He felt that it was such a grave disrespect for his son to refer to him by his nickname. He hung his head down, and gradually made his way to his bedroom. He wearily plopped down on his California king-sized bed.

CHAPTER 2
"A New Song?"

"SING UNTO THE LORD A NEW SONG"
PSALM 96:1A

Zachariah Phillips was busily preparing breakfast when Amoz sleepily entered into the spacious kitchen He wiped the sleep rheum from his eyes and grunted, "Good morning, Dad. You certainly were up kind of early for a Saturday."

Zachariah gingerly flipped the western omelet over in the oversized black cast iron skillet. "Morning, Amoz. I'm preparing your favorite, a western omelet with extra veggies."

"That's cool Dad, but I'm not really that hungry."

Zachariah carefully placed the omelet on a gilded edged plate. "You're not still upset with me about what happened the other day?"

"No Dad, I'm just not too hungry right now."

Zachariah earnestly tried to hide his disappointment. "No big deal, I'll just eat this delicious gourmet meal by myself. By the way, Amoz, would you do me a favor?"

Amoz paused and then replied, "Sure, what?"

Zachariah coughed a few times and then asked, "Would you go get the newspaper from out the driveway?"

Amoz complied with his father's request. He returned with the newspaper under his arm. There was some concern in his voice. "Dad, someone's park their car in our driveway. Do we have any guest here?"

Zachariah grinned, smiled broadly, and announced, "That's your car, son."

Amoz beamed, "Are you serious? A new BMW X6, and it's even in my favorite color—

"Yeah," Zachariah interjected. "Red." They both laughed and embraced each other. "Just imagine," Zachariah reminded Amoz. "When your parents died in that horrible car accident, and you were put up for adoption because there was no one to care for you. No family, no relatives, and the Lord blessed me to take you in."

Amoz still smiling, "Wow, those were some hard times. I was just about seven or eight. That's so true. I had no living relatives, and you took me in. I suppose that it was worth all the things that you and I went through. Wow, thanks Dad."

Zachariah reached into his pocket, pulled out an 18-karat gold chain with the initials, *'A.P.'* and dangled the key fob to the car in his hand. He tossed the key fob to Amoz. "Here, take it for a cruise. But first, eat this gourmet meal that I prepared for you."

Amoz took a few hurried bites and then declared, "I'll catch you later," he managed to say before slamming the door behind him.

An hour later as Zachariah sat at the grand piano working on a new song. Amoz returned with an ever-widening grin on his face. "Dad, this thing is sweet. It handles like a dream. Man, I mean this is too much."

Zachariah continued playing some chords and bass lines as he nodded his head in agreement. "I'm glad you like it."

"Like it? Are you serious? I love it! Dad, you're the greatest."

Zachariah again appeared to struggle for air, "Son, can you sing this refrain for me? I'm not feeling up to it right now."

"Your breathing is getting worse. It seems like this breathing thing really took off right after you received that letter from Yahweh's True Psalmist. I don't think this is a coincidence."

Amoz hummed along as his father played the melody. "Hey Dad, this song sounds remarkably familiar. Didn't I hear this before?" Amoz thought about it as his father played the requested refrain. "Wait a minute, Dad. This sounds like something from Prince. Wait, let me think. This sounds like the hook from *Little Red Corvette* or perhaps *Raspberry Beret.*"

Zachariah acknowledged, "Well, perhaps a little. Everybody borrows from everyone else in this music industry."

Amoz was now showing a little stress in his voice, "Dad, you've got to stop sampling other people's music. One day you're going to get sued like Marvin Gaye's family sued Pharrell Williams and Robin Thicke."
Zachariah continued playing, "Son, nobody sues God's people when they create music to praise Him."

Well "Dad," Amoz interjected. "I hope you didn't contact that Samuels guy about your convention. I mean Dad, don't let this guy hear this song. He'll hear Prince and *Little Red Corvette* instead of..." His voice trailed off and then restarted, "By the way what is the name of this song that you're writing?"

Zachariah paused playing the piano, "I'm calling it *'Let's Just Praise His Name.* Just relax, I'm only sampling a little bit of the song. I'm going to have you sing lead, and Wilson Paulie do a saxophone solo. Trust me, it will be great. It's going to be a hit at the convention."

Amoz reluctantly agreed, "Well okay Dad if that's what you think is best. But if I were you— "

11

Zachariah interrupted, "Don't be too concerned. Everybody is sampling somebody. I've been doing this for over thirty years. It's no big deal."

A few hours later Amoz invited some of his friends to take a spin in his new car. By this time Zachariah had completed composing and arranging his song. He decided it was time to contact several security agencies for 24-hour bodyguard protection. When he obtained what he thought would be the best security protection for him and his son, he picked up the phone and called Timothy Samuels. "Hello, is this Timothy Samuels?"

"Yes, how may I help you?" Timothy somehow managed to grunt into the phone.

"Timothy, my name is Zachariah Phillips and I want you to cover my Gospel music convention and do some investigations regarding the other artists that will be at the convention."

"Zachariah Phillips?" Timothy inquired. "I don't think I ever heard of you."

Zachariah voice indicated that he was a little perturbed. "I'm a Gospel recording artist. I got your number from your uncle, Bishop Graystien. Most people know me as the

Emperor of Gospel Music. I've been in the business for years."

Timothy's mind was a bit fuzzy as he tried to sound sympathetic. "Well, I'm not really that much into Gospel music. Wait a minute, let me think. I remember years ago my mother used to listen to your music. Did you have a song out about twenty years ago I think it was called *'Some Day I Am Going There'*? My mom played that song to death until, well her death. Now that she's dead, I guess she finally made it there. Wherever *there* may be." Timothy was unaware that Zachariah had merely taken an old public domain hymn by someone named Mrs. C.H. Morris., and rearranged it with a few modern chords. It was among his first big successes. The song even crossed over to the secular world and initiated his realm into royalty, as the Emperor of Gospel Music.

Zachariah was a little taken back that Timothy was oblivious to the fact that he is known as the Emperor of Gospel Music. However, he was a little pleased at the fact that Timothy probably didn't have a preference in Gospel music and would be a fair and even-handed reporter for his Gospel Performers Of the World Convention (G-POW). "Okay Timothy, I need to hire you to cover the G-POW Convention? You see, Brother Timothy, many of us Gospel artists have been receiving some disturbing emails, and text messages from some character who calls himself, *Yahweh's True Psalmist*." Zachariah waited for a reply from Timothy

13

who was contemplating what to say. "Timothy, are you still there?"

"Yeah man, I'm here. Can I get back to you with an answer? What's your number? Your number didn't show up on caller ID."

"Look Timothy, I've been having some privacy and security issues, Zachariah said. "Is it alright if I call you back in a few hours so you can think about it?"

Timothy was becoming skeptical about taking on this assignment, but he really needed some finances. "Well okay, Mr. Phillips. Just one quick question? Where and when is this convention taking place?"

Zachariah, once again was finding it somewhat difficult to catch his breath, but he managed to say, "It's in three weeks in Cincinnati."

"Solid man, I'll wait for your call." They both ended their conversation with dashes of doubt and apprehension for each other. Timothy chuckled to himself that a great Gospel singer would appear to be taken back or upset about receiving a message from another phony religious nut who calls himself 'Yahweh's True Psalmist'.

Chapter 3

"A Self-Made Pit"
"HE MADE A PIT, AND DIGGED IT,
AND IS FALLEN INTO THE DITCH WHICH HE MADE." PSALM 7:15

Timothy Samuels laid sprawled across the bed totally ignoring the buzzing of his phone as it vibrated on his cluttered desk. The phone call could have very well been from Zachariah Phillips, but he just did not want to talk to anyone. He had waited several hours for Zachariah to phone him. *'Perhaps,"* he thought. *"Mr. Phillips hired somebody else."*

It seemed as though the incessant buzz of the phone had permeated his spinning brain and was now intruding into the very marrow of his bones. He was determined not to answer the phone right at this moment. Nothing could deter him from escaping the realities of his wretched world.

His world was falling apart, and he felt as though it might have been because of his incompetency. How could he have been so naïve and plain too stupid to get hooked on drugs for the first time in his life? His life had become a total and complete fiasco of stupidity and utter selfishness.

He was quite disappointed regarding his relationship with his daughter, Teresa. His daughter was having her own issues with her newly acquired stepfather and the feelings of being neglected by her mother who had just given birth to a son. The last time Timothy that spoke to his daughter he was in a confused state of mind. This was no doubt due to the drug demon that had somehow taken possession of him. Teresa was a teenager with all the added drama of feeling left out by her own mother, and the lack of real support from her father. The last thing she needed was to be shackled with the chains of a drug addicted daddy.

He was also extremely frustrated with his love life – or the lack of a real love life. He had allowed himself, or perhaps permitted himself to fall victim of Cupid's unjust arrows. He thought that he would never again be too attached to another woman. However, he had fallen in love with Karen, and the very thing that he admired most about her, had become an albatross around his neck. She was one of those *church* girls. He felt that she was no loose woman; she was no Jezebel; she was a holy and righteous woman. Just the type of sanctified woman that would keep him on the straight and narrow path.

Yes, Karen was a so-called '*saved*'' girl with remarkably high morals that were beginning to impede upon his continuing increasing desires for a more physical relationship, as opposed to a spiritual relationship. He had become somewhat of a believer in this spiritual connection, but lately his desires had gradually become focused more on a sexual need. His spirit was once willing, but now his flesh had become entirely too weak. Karen was firm in her belief that pre-marital sex was a grave sin. Her first born child was born out of wed lock and she would not yield to that temptation again. She would not make the same mistake again and have a conjugal relationship without the full benefits of marriage. The weight of his desires and apparent aggressive advances toward her had caused her to erect a solid wall or a boundary that he couldn't breakdown or see his way through. '*Perhaps,*' he began to reason, '*she was just as sanctimonious as his daughter's step-father*'.

All these pressures were mounting, and Timothy had to find a way to escape his morbid reality. Timothy must have known that he was probably responsible for the pit that he had dug for himself. His mind was spinning in circles as he tried to ascertain how the Devil had tricked him into getting hooked on OxyContin. Yes, it was all the Devil's fault. He certainly wasn't going to blame it on Jesus, whom he had once thought to be his Savior. He began to ponder how could Jesus be his Savior and allow him to get hooked on this opioid? No, he wouldn't blame this mess on Jesus this time.

There had to be someone to pin the blame on - besides himself. He knew that he was becoming hooked and wanted desperately, but reluctantly to move on to heroin. He was neglecting his photography business, his blog and the assignments from his uncle, Bishop Graystien. Most importantly, he was neglecting his daughter. He began to rationalize and come up with excuses for all the people that he had let down. To make matters worse, his meager funds were all but depleted.

His confused and perplexed mind tried to review the steps and events that led to this dreadful situation. He had to blame someone, other than himself. The cloudy details of the origin of this situation began to formulate in his mish-mashed mind.

The ice storm that had begun a few months ago just exasperated him and brought his entire life into a tailspin. Yes, it was the ice storm's fault. After all, who causes ice storms? Mother Nature, of course. So, it must have been Mother Nature's fault. If he wouldn't blame himself, maybe he could throw some of the blame on Mother Nature. Since everyone knows that Mother Nature is actually God, he rationalized, then God was the culprit who formed the ice storm. The dreaded ice that covered the steps of the row house that he and his Aunt Sarah shared.

He vaguely remembered Aunt Sarah, saying, or perhaps pleading, "Now Tim, go out there and chop that ice, and don't forget to put salt on the steps and the sidewalk."

"Yes, ma'am," he mumbled as he headed for his room upstairs to edit some pictures for his blog.

'*Yes,*' he concluded. '*It was God's fault, and my aunt's fault. It was also Karen's nunnery approach to love that put me in this box. It must have been my daughter's mama's fault. It must have been my daughter's sanctimonious stepdad's mistreatment of my daughter. If I don't chill and calm myself, I'll end up hurting that dude. It must have been somebody, other than me. After all, who told my old behind aunt to go out there and try to remove that ice? After all, didn't I tell her that I would do it?*' Timothy simply wouldn't admit that he had neglected to take care of the ice in a timely fashion. He was beginning to conclude that after all his deliberating, that it ultimately might be God's fault. '*He caused the ice storm. Who told my senile Aunt Sarah that she had to go shopping for some outdated junk from the local bodega? After all, didn't I tell her that I would get rid of the ice? There she was trying to maneuver down those slippery steps. The next thing I knew; I heard her screaming in pain. She had fallen down the steps and broke her rusty old ankle. Yes, she's a little senile – God knew she was losing some of her mental faculties. Yes, who needs a God that doesn't look out for a golden saint like my dear old precious Aunt Sarah?*'

Aunt Sarah's ear-piercing shriek of distress caused Timothy to rush down from his second-floor room and try to aid his aunt. He almost slipped on the slimy slippery steps as he

18

attempted to pick her up. "Don't move me!" Screamed his aunt. "Dial the ambulance." He shot back into the house and grabbed the house phone and quickly dialed 911. He covered his aunt with his coat and a blanket to keep her warm and comfortable until the paramedics arrived.

He recalled how apologetic he was at first, and how he eagerly attended to his aunt's every need and request. He had to admit that his aunt took the entire episode in stride. "Well son," she would remind him. "It could have been worse. I only broke my ankle. The Lord spared me. I could have broken my hip. At my age, breaking a hip, or any other bone could mean the end of my life. It could mean going to a nursing home, but God spared me."

"You know you're right, Auntie." He remembered saying. "But this is all my fault. I should have put that rock salt out when you told me."

"Oh Tim," she would gently remind, "I know you've been busy. I should not have gone out there on the ice.

"I should have been more diligent in my responsibilities," Timothy insisted.

Aunt Sarah would simply smile, pat him on his head and say, "The Lord is yet good. I'm in some pain, but it could have been worse. The doctor gave me these pills, but I believe God, and I ain't taking them."

"Auntie," Timothy insisted, "You should take them. God gave the doctors knowledge to make medicine, so we don't have to suffer."

19

"I know Tim, but Jesus is my doctor, and He is my medicine," she said. She then handed him the pills and said, "Put this mess in the trash can. Timothy reluctantly took the pills from her, placed them in his pocket and eventually placed them in a drawer in his room. He reasoned that she might need them later. Timothy initially felt that it was his fault that his aunt had broken her ankle

. He was growing increasingly more agitated regarding the treatment that he felt his daughter was receiving by her mother and stepfather. He also had gotten behind in his child support payments, and he didn't want to be hassled by Cecelia, Teresa's mother. It seemed to him that every time he would visit his daughter, Cecelia would bring up some unnecessary drama which precipitated into arguments. He also felt uncomfortable being around her sanctimonious, self-righteous, and phony husband. He didn't need a spiritual discernment to understand that the Right Reverend Mickus, his daughter's stepfather, was the proverbial snake in the grass - directly from the Garden of Eden.

There was a great deal of internal pressure because of the neglect that he believed had led to his aunt's injury. In addition to that, there was his apparent neglect of the obvious needs of his daughter in an extremely critical time in her life. His finances and his life seemed to be totally out of his control. All these things mounted and piled up inside of him and he needed to find an escape. He had to remove himself from reality. He had to find a place to escape the pressures of life. He looked around his solitary room as though he was spying to see if anyone was looking over his shoulder. He slid his dresser drawer open and glided several of the OxyContin capsules into his eager and trembling lips, closed his eyes and slipped away into oblivion.

A few days after his aunt's mishap she called him. "Timothy, I need those pills. Did you throw them away? I didn't think you would really throw them away."

"Why Auntie," he mumbled. "You know that I always listen to you."

Aunt Sarah moaned a little, "Timothy, you and I know, and Jesus knows that you don't always listen to anybody."

"Are you in pain?" He queried and then sarcastically quipped, "I thought you said you would depend on Jesus."

"Well," Aunt Sarah insisted. "Well, I don't have a Balm in Gilead down here. I ain't in heaven to pluck a leaf from the Tree of Life. So, you bring me one of them pills if you haven't thrown them away like I asked you to do."

Timothy knew that he had squirreled away the pills. He reasoned that he needed them more than she would. "To be truthful, Auntie, I still have them. I kept them for you just in case your pain became unbearable." He went upstairs into his bathroom and filled her OxyContin prescription bottle with Tylenol capsules. He placed the OxyContin into the Tylenol bottle and placed that bottle into his pocket. He called out, "I'll be right down in a minute with the medicine."

'Aunt Sarah never really put all her faith in the pain pills,' he thoughtfully reasoned. *'So, Brother Doctor Jesus and Tylenol would do the trick for her, and the OxyContin would take care of my needs and do the trick for me'.*

Her doctor refilled the prescriptions as requested by his aunt. Timothy confiscated the prescription for his personal trips away from reality. The Tylenol somehow provided some comfort to her, Perhaps, it was a placebo effect – or her faith in Jesus. Or maybe, a combination of Jesus and the placebo. Timothy called the gradual healing the '*Jesus-placebo*' effect. The OxyContin managed to fulfil his needs. As she requested more pills from her doctor, Timothy would eagerly again escape reality by substituting her pills with Tylenol and ride high in the sky on her prescription of opioids. He was quite oblivious to the bleak and dangerous pit that he had dug for himself. He managed to continue this deception for several months. As for Aunt Sarah, *Jesus-placebo* was working quite nicely.

Chapter 4

"Steps"

"HOLD UP MY GOINGS IN THE PATH,
THAT MY FOOTSTEPS NOT SLIP" PSALM 17:5

Timothy felt that he had finally reached rock bottom – he hadn't answered any phone calls for the past several days. His confused mind tried to calculate how much money he would have made if he had only picked up the phone. He reasoned that he blew the assignment covering the G-POW convention.

He finally realized that the only way he could overcome his dependency on his drugs was to go cold turkey; and perhaps a little prayer might help. So, he made himself a prisoner in his room, refusing to talk to anybody, and ate very little food. He didn't even bother to shower or shave.

He wouldn't even listen to any music, except for a few tracks by Curtis Mayfield, Marvin Gaye, and Bobby Womack. He looped 'Flying High in the Friendly Sky', by Marvin Gaye. The Marvin Gaye's lyrics *'I'm hooked my friend to that boy that makes slaves out of men'* applied to him.

Curtis Mayfield's lyrics, *'Ain't nothing said, 'cause Freddy's dead'* seemed to paint a picture of his situation. Everything in his life seemed to be dead.

'Harry Hippie' by Bobby Womack's hook of, *'He's like a bottle in water...Harry just floats around'* described his existence. He felt as though he was just floating in a polluted ocean without any sign of land in sight.

For three straight days, 24 hours a day, he listened to these three cuts repeatedly. He felt that the lyrics of these songs, and a few sincere mumbled prayers would have cleansed his body and soul from his addiction. This routine was his current sincere form of church.

Early in the morning of the fourth day of this ordeal, he thought he was beginning to hallucinate. He tossed and turned in his sweat soaked bed as he heard voices from his daughter pleading for him to get himself together. He could hear his Uncle's voice of disappointment echoing in his inner ear. He could feel his girlfriend Karen's briny tearful kisses upon his dry parched lips.

In spite of the hallucinations, he was somewhat relieved that he no longer was waking up with a bed saturated with tears and especially sweat. He was also satisfied that his insomnia had finally subsided. He was managing his increased anxiety to his own satisfaction but was struggling to control the ease in which even the mundane things and events agitated him greatly. The final hindrance to what he felt was a complete recovery, was the feeling that he had ultimately conquered his bouts with diarrhea.

He could even imagine himself hearing Aunt Sarah slowly creeping up the stairs to his apartment. He imagined her knocking loudly on his door and calling out his name. He mumbled to himself, *'This ain't real. Aunt Sarah has never come up those steps, and besides, she's not able to climb any steep stairs.'*

The knocking on the door increasingly became louder and her calling his name seemed to be so real. In actuality, his Aunt Sarah was indeed banging on the door. "Tim! Tim, are you alright? Boy, do you hear me?"

Timothy still couldn't ascertain reality from fantasy, but he managed to reply, "Is that you, Aunt Sarah?"

"Boy, who else would it be? Open this door."

Timothy slowly rolled out of bed, and gradually cracked the door open and peered wearily at his aunt. He wasn't expecting to see anyone – and especially not his aunt. When he cracked the door open, Aunt Sarah abruptly forced her way into the room. "Timothy, what is wrong with you? My Lord in heaven, this place stinks."

Timothy rubbed his eyes and plopped himself on his bed. "Aunt Sarah?" He somehow formed his lips to say.

Aunt Sarah wagged her finger at the astonished young man as only she could do. "Who else were you expecting? This room is a mess. You're a mess. My Lord! Boy, do you stink.

What in the world have you been doing for the past week? I've been calling you. Your uncle has been trying to reach you. Your daughter, and even your so-called girlfriend has even contacted me to get a hold of you. What is going on?"

Timothy realized that his aunt was not an illusion or a mirage. She was actually in his room. She had rarely been in his room since he moved in several years ago. He wondered, and then asked, "Auntie, how did you get up the stairs?"

His aunt was more than eager to testify how she managed to get up the stairs. "Timothy, the Lord healed me. You hear that? He healed me. The doctor said that I'm almost completely recovered from my little injury. If you had been down to see me once in a while, you would have known that."

Timothy searched his mind for some excuse or rational to give his aunt. He could only mutter, "I haven't been feeling well. I think I might have the flu."

"Well," his aunt proclaimed in an unusually loud manner, "If you tried some prayer, the Lord would heal you of this flu, or whatever it is that you have. You see, son, he guided my footsteps. Oh, He's a healer."

Timothy just wanted to patronize her so he could finish his pity-party. He wanted to somehow get some much-needed sleep and finish his self-rehabilitation. "Well, Aunt Sarah. I think I feel better now."

Aunt Sarah quickly snapped back. "I know; I've been praying for you. I've been singing and praying and fasting. And I – "

Timothy interrupted her, "Thanks, but I just need to get some sleep right now."

She ignored his obvious hints that she should leave and sat on the bed next to him. Then gently held his hand and said, "The Lord has a blessing for you. Did you know that I got a call from the Emperor of Gospel Music, Zachariah Phillips?"

Timothy rubbed his eyes and focused them onto his aunt. "You mean that Gospel singer?"

Aunt Sarah seemed somewhat surprised that Timothy did not utterly understand how much weight and influence Zachariah Phillips had in the Gospel music world. "He told me to tell you that if you still want the assignment, you should call him today. If you don't contact him today, he will contact someone else. Since you are behind in your rent—"

"I'm working on that, Auntie. I'll have the back-rent money real soon."

Aunt Sarah continued. "And since you are behind in your child support payments, I suggest you get yourself together and call Zachariah. I left my chicken in the oven, so I've got to go and check on it." She slowly made an attempt to lift herself off the bed, and then insisted, "Just do me a favor, Tim."

Timothy attempted to help her up, but she refused his assistance. "Sure, anything for you."

"Well," his aunt stated as she gradually headed towards the door. "Actually, there's four favors that I need you to do."

Timothy replied with some hesitation. "Well, like I said, anything for you."

His aunt made it to the stairway and carefully placed her hand on the banister. "Number one, you need to pray. Number two take a shower, boy do you stink. Number three – call your daughter. And number four, call the Gospel Emperor, Zachariah. Oh, and there is one more thing."

Timothy rolled his eyes. "Now that makes five favors, Aunt Sarah"

His aunt grinned, "I can count. I want you to come on downstairs for some chicken, hoecake bread, and collard greens, and a little potato salad. I don't think you've eaten my food for quite a while."

. "I'll be there as soon as I can get out of the shower."
Timothy watched as she carefully and gingerly made her
way down the steep narrow stairs.

Chapter 5

"Depart From Evil"

"DEPART FROM EVIL AND DO GOOD.
AND DWELL FOREVER MORE" PSALM 37:27

Timothy somehow managed to pull himself together enough to descend the stairs and ease himself into one of Aunt Sarah's kitchen chairs. Aunt Sarah smiled as she placed the piping hot plate in front of him. In actuality, the enticing aroma of the food merely increased the nauseous feeling that had made his stomach quiver which took all of his will power to prevent him from breaking wind.

Aunt Sarah continued to smile even though she showed mild disappointment in her eyes because Timothy merely stared at the food. "Is there something wrong with my cooking?" She asked him gently.

Timothy had to think of a way not to offend his aunt. "No Auntie, the food looks delicious. I'm just not feeling too well."

"Why don't you take a few bites." Aunt Sarah suggested. "It might make you feel better." Timothy sliced the chicken breast into small pieces and took a miniscule bite. "That's my boy," Aunt Sarah said. "Now, try a little bite of the collard greens."

30

Timothy took a small forkful of the well-seasoned greens and placed it into his mouth. He suddenly managed to excuse himself from the table and dashed into the bathroom. He had not quite conquered what he thought was his final withdrawal battle – diarrhea.

"Timothy," Aunt Sarah summoned as she knocked on the bathroom door. "Are you alright?"

"I'm okay. I just need to go upstairs and rest."

"Okay. I'll wrap the food up and you can eat it later."

Timothy flushed the toilet, washed his hands, and gradually made it up the stairs to his room and broke out into a cold sweat as the world spun around in his head. He began to imagine or hallucinate that he heard his aunt calling his name out in prayerful moans.

Drenching in a cold sweat a few hours later, Timothy woke up to the buzzing of his phone vibrating on his dresser. He couldn't recall the last time he even bothered to glance at his phone or his computer. He felt compelled to read the latest text message that he received. *'Perhaps,'* he thought. *'It may be from my daughter; or maybe Zachariah Phillips still wants me to cover the convention.'* As he laid across the bed, he read the message: ***"Depart from evil, and do good; and dwell forever more."*** He tried to reason in his mind who would send such a message. *'Aunt Sarah doesn't text anybody. I don't think she even knows how. Neither would* *my uncle, Bishop Graystien'.* In bold type, he read the sender's name: **Yahweh's True Psalmist.** Though Timothy's mind was still somewhat disheveled, he vaguely remembered Zachariah Phillips mentioning Yahweh's True Psalmist. Timothy wondered why he was contacted by this Psalmist when Timothy wasn't a Gospel singer, and in fact barely could tolerate Gospel music. *'Perhaps,"* he thought. *'I better get myself together and get involved with this G-POW convention. After all, I've been given a calling card from Yahweh's True Psalmist, whoever or whatever that is.'*

Timothy Samuels wasn't the only person to have received a Scriptural message from the Psalmist recently. Zachariah Phillip's chief rival in the Gospel music royalty world is Joktan Jahnson, Jr. He was known throughout the Gospel music industry as Archduke Joktan. His contemporary style of music drew young people. He also reigned in older people, who thought they were young minded, to his concerts and church services in huge numbers.

The Emperor of Gospel Music disdain for Archduke Joktan was intensified when Archduke Joktan was crowned the *Archduke of Gospel Music* by the Gospel DJ Consortium. To Zachariah Phillip's way of thinking, there could be only one male royalty in the Gospel music world, and Zachariah would carry the title to his grave. Zachariah took pleasure in secretly teasing Archduke Joktan regarding his name. Joktan, is a Hebrew name which meant *'he will be made little'.* Zachariah also found it profoundly ironic that Archduke Joktan was at least 5 inches taller than he was. *'He might be taller than me in the physical realm'* Zachariah reasoned. *'But he will always be made little in the Gospel music realm.'*

With the death threats coming from Yahweh's True Psalmist, Zachariah reasoned that Archduke Joktan was the mastermind behind the entire incidents of threats and harassments carried out by *YAHWEH'S TRUE PSALMIST.* However, the Emperor was totally unaware to the fact that YAHWEH'S TRUE PSALMIST had almost every major Gospel artist nervous and apprehensive about attending the G-POW convention. Especially Archduke Joktan who had just received the following messages: *'Rivers of waters run down mine eyes, because they keep not the law. Psalm 119:136. Yahweh's True Psalmist'.* Archduke Joktan laughed at this message and reasoned that the Emperor himself, Zachariah had sent it. A few moments later the second message arrived: *'Then the proud waters had gone over our soul. Psalm 124:5 YAHWEH'S TRUE PSALMIST'.* The third and final message arrived that day a fraction of a second later. *'And the waters covered their enemies: there was not one of them left. Psalm 106:11 YAHWEH'S TRUE PSALMIST'.*

Archduke Joktan recalled that the Emperor was doing a live interview on one of the Christian stations at the very moment he received the cryptic text messages. Archduke Joktan pondered how could Zachariah send out three quick text messages and be live and in color on his television screen at the same time? *'Perhaps,'* he reasoned. *'This Yahweh's True Psalmist' is a real peril not just to me and other artists, but to the so-called Emperor as well.*

Chapter 6

"The Good Man"

COME, LET US TAKE OUR FILL OF LOVE UNTIL THE MORNING: LET US SOLACE OURSELVES WITH LOVES. FOR THE GOODMAN IS NOT AT HOME, HE IS GONE A LONG JOURNEY:" PROVERBS 7:18-19

Timothy felt that his crisis was finally, if not gradually receding. He felt that he had reached the point that he was competent enough to face the challenges of fighting his addiction demons and fulfilling his obligations. He called Zachariah Phillips and agreed to meet him tomorrow in Philadelphia to discuss arrangements, sign a contract, and receive a retainer.

"Listen Brother Timothy," Zachariah said as they were concluding their conversation. "I have to be honest with you."

"Yes Sir." Timothy responded giving his best effort to sound more professional than he did during their initial contact. "I wouldn't expect anything less from a man of God like yourself." Timothy added to perhaps butter up the man's apparent tremendous ego.

Zachariah continued. "I heard through your uncle, Bishop Graystien, that you have also received correspondence from Yahweh's True Psalmist. It's getting a little creepy – even for an anointed man of God such as myself. You better be prayed up, son."

Timothy started to make a scoffing response, but cunningly patronized him, "I will pray. My Aunt Sarah will be praying, and Bishop Graystien, and of course, you will too."

"Wait. Wait a minute." Zachariah interjected just before Timothy halted the call.

"I heard from the so-called 'Archduke of Gospel Music', Joktan Jahnson, Jr., better known as Archduke Joktan."

Timothy was totally bewildered, but managed to say, "Man, you guys really do have some titles. Sort of like bishops, reverends, popes, apostles, and so on."

Ignoring Timothy's response, Zachariah continued. "Archduke Joktan received some very strange messages from this Yahweh's True Psalmist."

Timothy was genuinely anxious about this particular message. "Well, what did the message say?"

To heighten the suspense, the Emperor of Gospel Music merely indicated, "His email is ArchdukeJoktan@G-POW.org. He will fill you in."

Archduke Joktan checked into the Hotel Roanoke & Conference in Virginia without his usual entourage, close friends, or his wife. He had informed his wife that he was going to be in Manhattan working on a project with a new unrecorded Gospel hip hop artist. He briskly made his way to the luxury suite and eagerly waited in anticipation for an important phone call.

He had been corresponding secretly with concealed lovers for years, and he was especially delighted and deliriously aroused by his newest encounter with Lomonsha. They had met recently on an internet chat site. After several days of planning, he had finalized the details for an intimate hookup. He was tantalized by Lomonsha's ability to thrill him in messages. He also was virtually mesmerized by the beauty as shown in the profile photos she had sent to his private e-mail. The images indicated to him that Lomonsha was no doubt a flawless beauty queen. His desire – and the straightforward lust they expressed to each other, urged the two to meet as soon as feasible. To Archduke Joktan, the most viable and workable time had ultimately arrived.

As he unpacked his overnight bag, he glanced at his phone as it indicated he had a text message. With great excitement and some apprehension, he began to read the following message: '*Come, let us take our fill of love until the morning; let us solace ourselves with loves.*' His heart was actually palpitating at this message from the lover he was expecting at any given moment. Before he even read the rest of the message, he promptly strolled over to the deep heart-shaped sunken tub and began to fill it with water and solution to make mounds of bubbles. As the water gently flowed into the tub, he continued reading the message. '*For the good man is not a home, he is gone a long journey.*' He was equally excited about this portion of the message. Finally, he managed to focus on the final part: '*Proverbs 7:18-19 Son of the Yahweh's True Psalmist.*' He could not believe or comprehend this bizarre and outlandish message. Especially now that he was so anxious about his rendezvous with Lomonsha.

He was bewildered. He tried to reason who was the Son of the True Psalmist. He concluded that if David wrote the book of Psalms, and if his son, Solomon is credited for writing Proverbs, perhaps there is more than one person who is Yahweh's True Psalmist. He further reasoned that the True Psalmist might be a group of disenchanted fools or even a copy-cat trying to emulate the True Psalmist.

However, he wasn't going to let anyone ruin his pre-planned hookup with his incandescent lover. He was somewhat startled when his phone rang. He was, however, relieved to see Lomonsha's number on the screen of his I-phone. "Hey, baby." He said in a voice hiding any tell-tale stress.

"Yes, Joktan, baby. I should be up in a few moments." Lomonsha said in a coy-like fashion.

Archduke Joktan always had an aggressive, yet cryptic and covert reputation as a lover, and tonight would not be the exception. "Lomonsha girl, I'll leave the door unlock. I'll

be soaking in our heart-shaped tub as we planned, and I can't
wait until you get here."

Lomonsha's voice seemed to purr as a hat was pulled down
on the well coiffured head. Lomonsha entered the elevator.
"I can't wait, baby. Just hold on, I'm on my way up."

Archduke Joktan relaxed and leaned back as the bubbles
floated up to his neck. This bathtub rendezvous had been
planned during their last correspondence. A few moments
later he could hear the door open as Lomonsha entered the
suite and then locked the door. He smiled as Lomonsha
ostentatiously approached him as he laid sprawled out and
completely relaxed in a sea of soap bubbles. He pivoted his
head to get a better glance. "Lomonsha, come on in, the
water is fine, but not as fine as you, baby."

Lomonsha slowly entered the room. "I've been waiting so
long for this moment." Lomonsha said in a low seductive
and enticing voice.

Archduke Joktan sighed loudly, "I can't wait another
minute." He then insisted, "But baby, you can't get in the
tub like that. You know how we both plan this whole thing.
I'm ready for the real deal. Now, come on, baby. Let's get
it on."

Lomonsha placed her hands on his shoulders and whispered
gently into his ear. "Let me give you a little massage first,
and then a special message straight from my heart."

39

Archduke Joktan closed his eyes and moaned, "Here I am baby, do what you want."

Lomonsha's well-manicured hands began to gently massage his shoulders, and then whispered. "You're getting the massage. How does that feel, baby?" Archduke Joktan didn't utter a word; he just moaned as the massage became more intense.

Lomonsha's voice purred liked a well contented cat. "And now, I'll give you the message." She leaned over and ever so smoothly whispered gently into his ear. "The good man is not home; he is gone a long journey!" Archduke Joktan was totally shocked to hear the very words that were texted to him by Yahweh's True Psalmist. As Archduke Joktan tried to spin around in the tub, Lomonsha forced his head under water. The more he struggled to be released, the tighter the grip seemed to be. Lomonsha finally released the hold. Lomonsha snatched his head above water as he gasped desperately for air. He was too weak to respond to the sharp blows delivered across both of his cheek. Water mingled with blood rocketing from his face and splattered onto the walls as he was continually walloped from side to side by the vicious blows delivered by his intended lover. He was totally humiliated and embarrassed. His mind was too befuddled to think of anything to say as Lomonsha seemed to glide away as if on skates. Lomonsha left the room without hesitation and quickly boarded the elevator as Joktan stumbled and fell repeatedly back into the tub several times. He was too weak and too naked to try and pursue her. By the time he made his way to the bedroom to put on a robe, Lomonsha had driven several miles away. Lomonsha removed a wig, threw it in the back seat of the car. Then the make-up was wiped from the face and false eyelashes were plucked off. Finally, as the car approached the interstate, fake finger manicured nails were thrown on the floor of the car.

Archduke Joktan couldn't call 911 without exposing his behavior to his fans who looked up to him. However, his greatest fear was for his wife to discover this affair, sue him for divorce and collect nice alimony checks for a long time. Actually, Lomonsha could never be accurately described or apprehended because Lomonsha was actually Yahweh's True Psalmist. Lomonsha was a monster, and as Yahweh's True Psalmist, **he** knew emphatically that he would be the only '*Goodman*' at the Gospel Performers of the World Convention.

Chapter 7

"Forsaken Child"

"When My Father and My Mother Will Forsake Me,
The Lord Will Take Me Up" PSALM 27:10

Timothy hurriedly packed his digital cameras into his bag and prepared to place his wide-angle fish-eye lens in its pouch. As he placed the lens into the pouch, he noticed that there was something at the bottom of the custom-made sack. He emptied the pouch out and discovered a forgotten stash of his OxyContin pills. He decided to escort his former friends to the toilet and flush them into eternity, but something compelled him to wrapped them in toilet tissue and place them back into several old 35-millimeter film canisters. *'I might have a relapse,"* he reasoned. *'I think I've conquered this monkey on my back, but just in case, I'll hold on to these bad boys.'* He finished loading his camera equipment, grabbed his garment bag, and the rest of his luggage and bounded down the stairs.

He tapped lightly on Aunt Sarah's door. She knew it was her nephew and smiled broadly as she walked out to meet him. He realized that in spite of all his missteps and faults, she would always be in his corner, and more importantly, she would pray for him. "Now Tim, you take the Lord with you. I'll be praying for you."

Timothy knew that she was sincere, so he decided not to be sarcastic or condescending. "I love you Auntie," was all that he could say without sounding too sentimental. "Do you remember when you use to talk to me about being a good little boy?"

Auntie Sarah rubbed his head as she nodded. "I remember. Now you're a man."

Timothy smiled as he headed out the door. "Well Auntie, I promised to be working on being good. I'll really try, I promise." Timothy slowly walked out the door and down the stairs. "I've got to go, the limo's here."

"One more thing, Timothy Samuels." Aunt Sarah said as she followed him out to the sidewalk. "The steps of a good man are ordered by the Lord. And a good man is also a good father. Call your daughter because she's been trying to reach you."

As the limo driver opened the door for Timothy, he waved and said, "I will. I promise. Bye." He entered the rear of the spacious car as the driver loaded his luggage. He leaned back in the well-padded seat, lowered the window, and waved a final good-bye to his aunt.

Timothy tried to make small talk with the driver as he entered the Pennsylvania Turnpike. The driver indicated that he was Zachariah Phillips' personal driver and one of the newly hired bodyguards. Zachariah felt he needed more security due to the apparent threats of Yahweh's True Psalmist. Timothy abruptly ended his chat with the driver when he realized that he had to call his daughter. "Excuse me, sir. I've got to make a quick call."

He closed the partition glass between him and the driver to have a private conversation with his daughter. He felt some guilt and anxiety as the phone indicated an incoming call from Zachariah Phillips. "Hello, Mr. Phillips, thanks for providing this ride."

Zachariah chuckled, "You don't have to be so formal, just call me Zachariah. I hope the ride is comfortable. And speaking of rides, I've rented a car for you. It will be available right after we meet and have our talk."

Timothy smiled and replied, "Thanks, I really appreciate it."

"No problem," Zachariah responded. "You'll need the car to make a trip to Brooklyn tomorrow and then on to Gary, Indiana."

Trying to show some composure, Timothy queried, "Brooklyn? New York?" Timothy knew that the only way to get to Brooklyn from almost anywhere was to cross a bridge. He was terrified of driving across bridges. His gephyrophobia – or fear of bridges would certainly be tested if he had to cross over the Brooklyn Bridge, Manhattan Bridge, or especially, the Verrazano-Narrows Bridge.

Zachariah asked, "Is there a problem with you going to Brooklyn? I know that you are not afraid of being in the 'hood. After all, you've travelled all across this country taking pictures."

Timothy took a deep, but silent breath. "No sir. It's cool." He was not really being truthful as he continued. "I know all about Brooklyn, Manhattan, Queens, Staten Island, and the Bronx. No problem at all."

Zachariah Phillips continued, "Great. Then you can interview a brother that's really on the cutting edge of Gospel music today, especially Hip-Hop Gospel Music."

Timothy responded, "You mean to tell me that there is something called 'Hip-Hop Gospel Music'? Man, that's kind of shot out to me?"

Zachariah let out a loud guffaw. "You don't know much about Gospel Music, do you? That's probably the precise reason why I knew you would be perfect for the job. Man, there's all genres of Gospel music crossing every style and genre. There's even--"

He interrupted Zachariah in mid-sentence as his phone buzzed indicating that his daughter was on the other line. "Look Zachariah, my daughter is on the other line. Is it alright if I get back to you?"

"No problem," Zachariah quipped. "I'll fill in the details when you get here." Zachariah ended the call as Timothy proceeded to respond to his daughter.

Timothy's voiced beamed as he said, "Hey, Teresa."

Timothy was shocked at the tone of his daughter's voice as she grunted, "Dad, why do sound so happy? How can you be that happy? I haven't heard from you in weeks and weeks. You act as though I don't even exist. You act as if I don't have any feelings."

Timothy tried to explain, "You see baby, I've been going through a lot of stuff. You don't understand."

Without missing a beat, Teresa asserted, "Dad, I've been going through some stuff too. I have issues that you don't know about. Maybe if you had called once in a while, you would know what's happening in my life."

"Well, I'm sorry," Timothy admitted trying to be as sympathetic as possible.

Teresa continued to speak in harsh tones. "Yeah, Dad. Sorry doesn't have anything to do with it. Sorry just doesn't cut it anymore. I'm your only child. I've got issues, some real serious issues."

"Okay, baby. I'm here for you now. What's going on?"

Timothy could feel her emotion as her voice began to quiver. Timothy could also sense the pain as she said, "I need you so much, Daddy. I can't take this anymore. Maybe it would be better if I lived with you and Aunt Sarah. That's what I want to know. I want to live with you and Auntie Sarah. My mother and my stepfather only seem to care about the baby and church. I feel like I'm a stranger in this house. I'm treated like dirt."

Trying to cheer her up, Timothy said, "Now, don't exaggerate. It can't be that bad. Do you think that you might be jealous of the baby?"

Teresa asserted firmly, "I am not jealous of the baby. I love my baby brother. I just can't stand his father. He actually wants me to call him 'Daddy'. They don't understand that you are the only daddy I know. And lately, I haven't even known you. Besides that, he looks at me kind of funny. You know what I mean? I don't trust that man one tiny bit."

Timothy's voice began to show some genuine concern. "What do you mean, 'he looks at you kind of funny'?"

"Now Dad, don't act like you are so naïve. You know exactly what I mean. It's like he's sort of scoping on me. He's checking me out by looking me up and down, like he's undressing me with his eyes."

Timothy avoided yelling to the phone because he was concerned that the driver would hear his remarks. He

47

struggled to speak in soft even tones to calm himself down and bring some tranquility to his daughter. "Teresa, now tell me the truth. He hasn't tried anything with you, has he?"

Teresa assured him, "No Dad, of course not. It's just the way he looks at me. You know Dad, it's just a look. It's not easy to explain or describe."

"You don't have to worry about him anymore. I'm coming to pick you up as soon as I get done with my business in Philly. That's a promise. I'm taking you to Brooklyn because I have to interview a Gospel Hip Hop artist. I don't know his name, but you're coming with me."

Teresa was showing her inquisitiveness. "You don't know his name? I'm into Gospel Hip Hop. Is it Pos-I-tive Rhema?"

Timothy had to admit, "I don't know who it is. All I know is that I will see you tomorrow. And that jive preacher better not lay his hands on you. He's a sanctimonious, fake-behind, jive preacher punk. I don't want to go to jail for hurting somebody."

Teresa relaxed a little at the encouraging words of her father and laughed softly. "Don't worry, Dad. He won't be trying anything with me. I remember some of the Kung Fu you use to teach me."

"Solid," Timothy said as he concluded the call. "I'll pick you up tomorrow. Get your things packed and tell your mother that I don't want to hear jack from her. I don't want to hear a thing from anybody because I'll go off on everybody. You hear me? I mean that. You're coming with me tomorrow and then to the Gospel Performers of the World Convention in Cincinnati."

Teresa voice displayed a little spark. "Thanks, Dad. I love you so much."

Timothy sighed. "Yeah, baby. I love you even more."

Chapter 8

"Crooked And Bent Out Of Shape"

"THAT WHICH IS CROOKED CANNOT BE MADE STRAIGHT:
AND THAT WHICH IS WANTING CANNOT BE NUMBERED"
ECCLESIASTES 1:15

Zachariah Phillips took a long draw from his cigarette and held the smoke in his lungs for a few moments and then let it slowly ease out as he answered his phone. "Hey Amoz, what's up? You sound a little distressed."

Amoz's voice of anxiety and fear oozed through Zachariah's Beats headphones. "Dad, I received a text from The Son of Yahweh's True Psalmist this morning."

Zachariah removed the cigarette from his mouth and crushed it out with his foot. Trying to calm his son down, Zachariah assured, "Just relax son, everything is going to be alright. Now, tell me what was so upsetting about the message?"

Amoz's voice was still wreaking with distress. "Dad, it's not really about what he said."

"Come on Amoz, just relax. Take some deep breaths." Zachariah instructed him. "Are you breathing in slowly through your nose? Now start from the beginning and tell me what's wrong."

Amoz began his explanation with a mumbled response. "Dad, uhh well, uhh. You see I---"

"Come on now son, you've got to speak up. You're not making any kind of sense."

Zachariah could faintly hear his son make an audible sigh as he gathered his thoughts. "Dad, this morning I received a text from the Son of Yahweh's True Psalmist."

"You mean to tell me that now he has a son? Next thing you know, someone will be sending texts from Yahweh's sisters, brothers, cousins, and maybe even his grandmother. Listen, it's probably the same guy," Zachariah reasoned.

Amoz continued, "His quote came from the book of Ecclesiastes. Now, you know that if David is considered to be the Psalmist of the Bible, then his son Solomon, would logically be the Son of the Psalmist. After all, didn't Solomon write Proverbs, Ecclesiastes, and Song of Solomon? Am I right, Dad?"

"Well, I suppose so," Zachariah acknowledged. "Now tell me the message and what happened to make you so upset. It's not the first-time members of G-POW have received some of this devil's taunts."

Amoz agreed, "You may be right, but listen to this message and then I'll tell you what bothers me. The message was: *'That which is crooked cannot be made straight: and that which is wanting cannot be numbered. Ecclesiastes 1:15'*. It was signed, *Son of Yahweh's True Psalmist.*"

Zachariah let out a soft chuckle. "Do you mean to tell me that this ridiculous message has you so bent out of shape? My Lord son, where is your faith? These words shouldn't and couldn't hurt you, now could they?"

"It's not the words that hurt or bothered me. Let me explain. I went to Red Lobster for lunch. When I came out of the restaurant, all the tires on my new BMW truck were flatten. I mean flat as a pancake."

"Now Amoz, we have Triple A, and GEICO insurance, so what's the big deal?"

"Dad not only were the tires totally flat, but the wheels were bent out of shape. They were so crooked that they couldn't even be straightened out by the BMW mechanics. Just like the message said about the crooked not being able to be straight."

Zachariah's voice immediately fluctuated to show the impact of the situation. "How did you get home? Is everything alright?"

Amoz tried to reassure his father, when in truth, he wanted his father to reassure him. "Dad, it's all cool. I had the car towed, and I rented a little Chevy to get me home."

"That's great son, as long as you're okay. We'll get your car fixed. However, understand that we have an image to uphold, and we don't want my congregation and any of our Gospel followers to see us in a compromising position."

Amoz blurted, "What do you mean by a compromising position? Dad, do you mean if I'm not seen in a Benz or BMW, that means we're disappointing our church and our fan base? That puts us in a compromising position. A compromising position with who?"

Without a moment's hesitation, Zachariah reminded him. "After all, I have a prosperity ministry. I cannot proclaim the blessing of the Lord that we have if we don't show it. People don't often pay attention to a preacher's words. They only see what they want to see about him. The image of the preacher is not what he says or proclaims. It is what the people see. When they see us, they will see God's prosperity working in us and through us. They won't see that image in a Chevy or a Honda, or a Toyota. We have an image to uphold. So, get that car fixed ASAP and used the church's business account credit card."

With some hesitation Amoz said, "Solid Dad, I'll rent a Range Rover or either a Porsche until my BMW is repaired."

"That's sounds like prosperity to me." Listen Amoz," he said as he saw Timothy Samuels approaching him. "I have to hang up now. I see Brother Samuels coming towards me. I'll meet you in Cincinnati."

53

Zachariah wave to get the attention of his security guard who was standing within earshot. "Listen James, I need you to go to my house and keep an eye on my son. I should have never left him alone. You understand? He's received one of those messages and his car has been damaged. You go there and check it out."

James nodded, "Are you sure everything is going to be okay? Who's going to be here with you?"

"It's alright, I still have my driver Lamont. He'll fill in for you, after all, he is also on my security staff. It's cool, man." James left as Timothy approached and gave him a look of distrust.

Zachariah rose from his seat and shook Timothy's hand as he motioned for him to take a seat next to him. Zachariah instructed his driver to leave. "Lamont, you can just relax for a while. You can go back upstairs and watch some T.V. I need to talk to Brother Samuels privately."

Lamont inquired, "Mr. Phillips are you sure you can trust this guy?"

Zachariah and Timothy looked at each other in bewilderment as Zachariah squinted his eyes in disapproval of Lamont's remark. Lamont understood the gesture and went back into the hotel lobby.

Zachariah then focused his attention on Timothy. "How was your trip, Brother Tim?"

Timothy nervously smiled. "Just fine, Mr. Phillips. Thanks, everything went well. Now, how can I help you? Just what do you need me to do."

Zachariah lit another cigarette. "You don't mind if I smoke, do you Timothy? Also, you don't have to be so formal with me. I told you to call me Zachariah."

Timothy agreed, "It's okay about the smoking. I'll try to remember to call you Zachariah. I just wanted to give you your due respect. By the way, I understand your smoking, I used to smoke too." Timothy really didn't like being around people who smoked because it arouses his desire to go back and embrace the habit again.

"Tell me Timothy," Zachariah pondered. "How did you quit smoking? I've been trying on and off for years. I find it so hard to quit. I hear that the nicotine habit is harder than crack-cocaine."

Timothy didn't want to explain how he went from cigarettes to electronic cigarettes. He would be embarrassed to explain how some preacher prayed that he would be delivered from smoking. He still couldn't wrap his mind around a God helping him do something like kicking a habit. He felt that he had kicked his OxyContin habit through the church of Marvin Gaye's, Curtis Mayfield's, and Bobby Womack's music. Deep within the corner of his mind, he gave a little morsel of credit to his Aunt Sarah's prayers. "Well," he said. "I guess I was lucky."

"Man, you certainly don't put much faith in God. I've read your blogs and how you cover events, so I'll be straight up with you. I need you to be who you are. I don't care that you are skeptical about the church. Most of the major Gospel artists in our organization have been harassed by some character who calls himself, *'Yahweh's True Psalmist'*. Strange things have been happening. For example, my car was shot up. My son just told me that all his tires on his new car were damaged. Did you contact Archduke Joktan? Did he tell you what happened?" Zachariah stomach turned as he referred to Joktan as *Archduke*. He felt that he had to use the Archduke term because that's what most people called him.

Timothy shook his head. "He said something about being attacked while he was taking a bath, and how he almost drowned. He didn't give me any further details."

Zachariah continued. "Just before these events happened, cryptic Biblical passages were sent from the book of Psalms, Ecclesiastes, and Proverbs and Song of Solomon. All these books were written for the most part, either by David or his son, Solomon. Are you familiar with these Biblical patriarchs and their writings?"

Timothy leaned closer to Zachariah, trying to avoid the smoke emanating from his cigarette and softly confided, "Yeah, I used to go to Sunday School at my uncle's church. He's a bishop and I remember hearing about David and Goliath. I also remember about Solomon and Delilah. I have to admit to you that I also received a message from this Yahweh Psalm guy. I'm not a Gospel performer – in fact, I don't really care for most Gospel music. I don't know why I was contacted. Anyway, nothing has happened to me."

Zachariah touched him on his shoulder and stated, "Listen Timothy, I'm not disrespecting your Sunday School upbringing, but Solomon and Delilah don't quite go together. And regarding, the True Psalmist, I have to agree that nothing has happened to you yet. However, I wouldn't feel so comfortable. I also have to point out that every single major artist has received some type of message from this guy. That is everyone in our organization, except an extremely popular hip-hop Gospel artist."

Timothy interrupted, "Is this artist named Pos-I-tive Roomer?"

"You mean, Pos-I-tive Rhema," Zachariah corrected. "Have you heard of him? I thought you weren't really into Gospel music."

Timothy admitted, "No, I'm not into Gospel music at all. My daughter happened to mention his name some time ago. She says he's one of her favorite singers."

"I wouldn't call what he does, 'singing', but he is very popular with the younger crowd."

Timothy challenged him, "Do I sense a little jealousy on your part? I'm just being for real."

Zachariah insisted, "I'm being for real too. I am the number one Gospel Artist in the world. I am at the top of the Gospel realm – I am the Emperor. Naw man, I am certainly not jealous of him or anybody else. He has his little niche and I have my empire of niches. It's just odd that Pos-I-tive Rhema is probably the only person in our whole organization that has not been touch in any way, shape, or form by this clown psalmist. He's the only one that I know of. Now, are you up to the task? Can we depend on you?"

Zachariah and Timothy spent several hours discussing in detail the various artist that had received any strange messages from the Psalmist. Timothy also insisted that he should have contact information for everyone connected to the G-POW Convention.

Timothy thought about what had been discussed in detail and began to question whether or not he should take his daughter with him to Brooklyn and to the G-POW Convention. He wondered, *'If this guy is in fact a threatening perpetrator, I might be putting my daughter and my own safety in jeopardy.'*

Zachariah Phillips hadn't had a cigarette for the past several hours during the long discussions, and decided it was time to light up again. He took a deep drag, and then restated his questions. "Now, Brother Timothy Samuels, do you think you can handle the task and can I, or should I say, *we* depend on you?"

Timothy however, nodded in agreement, shook his hand and replied, "I'm on it, man. You can depend on me."

Chapter 9

"A Bed Far From Hades"

"FOR YOU WILL NOT LEAVE MY SOUL IN HELL,
NOR WILL YOU ALLOW YOUR HOLY ONE TO SEE CORRUPTION"
PSALM 16:10A

Timothy tuned his radio to the Philadelphia Gospel radio station, Praise 107.9, to familiarized himself with some of the artists he would no doubt meet at the convention. He listened to the various genres of Gospel music that he heard until the station finally drifted out of range as he cruised down the roadway. He was pleased that he managed to set up the Bluetooth system in the car provided, as well as downloaded all of his contacts.

He was quite relaxed as he passed the Quakertown, Pennsylvania exit on the Turnpike, when he answered the phone. The display on the dashboard indicated that it was from his uncle, Bishop Graystien. "Timothy, how are things going?" His uncle's voice boomed through the dashboard speakers.

"Fine, simply fine, Uncle – I mean, Bishop. Everything is cool."

Bishop responded, "I'm glad to hear that. I suppose you're on assignment for the upcoming Gospel Music Convention.

How are things going with your daughter? And how is Karen doing?"

Timothy's voice showed some hesitation in answering his uncle's questions, but he managed to reply, "They're both doing fine. In fact, I'm on my way to pick up my daughter in Harrisburg and then we're off to Brooklyn."

Bishop's voice modulated to indicate to Timothy that he wanted to make a very profound point, or pearl of wisdom. Timothy was all too familiar with that tone of voice and listened attentively. "Now Timothy, everybody knows how judgmental you can be."

"But Uncle – "

In an authoritarian tone, Bishop Graystien continued. "Don't judge the artists you may come across. Some of them might not appear to be sincere or even may be totally phony to you. Son let God be the judge. You just report what you see, and what you hear. Leave your prejudicial shenanigans out of your reporting. Don't stereotype everyone who render praises unto the Lord by any misbehavior of a few. Don't lump all the true worshippers of God with any shady or unsavory characters you might run across. Do you understand what I'm saying?"

"I understand, Uncle. I will do my best to be straight up and honest." Timothy wasn't exactly being candid with his uncle. In fact, he was thinking that perhaps his uncle, Bishop

Graystien may in fact be Yahweh's True Psalmist. Timothy knew that his uncle was a defender of the Faith and wouldn't tolerate any foolishness on the part of anyone who was playing church and especially when it came to the worship and praise of the Lord. Timothy gradually and momentarily dismissed this thought from his mind because he knew that Bishop Graystien would not involve himself in harming anyone.

Bishop Graystien concluded his remarks by saying, "I will probably see you in Cincinnati at the G-POW convention. Oh Timothy, one more thing. Please call your Aunt Sarah when you hang up from me. Have you reached the Allentown Exit yet? If not, you'd better stop by her house."

Timothy protested, "Uncle, I don't have time to go by there, get to Harrisburg, and then make it to Brooklyn tonight. Teresa and I had planned to stay at a hotel in Jersey City or either Hoboken."

Bishop Graystien insisted, "Just call your aunt and she'll explain everything."

Timothy agreed as they both ended the call. He voice-dialed his aunt's number. "Hello, Aunt Sarah. Bishop Graystien wanted me to call you."

Timothy was a little startled when he realized that it wasn't his aunt's voice that had responded. "Hello Daddy," Teresa said. She didn't get a response. Timothy was at a loss for words. "Daddy, are you still there?"

Timothy managed to say, "Teresa, I think I miss-dialed. I thought I was calling your Aunt Sarah."

Teresa grinned, "Daddy, you're so crazy. You didn't miss-dial, I'm over Aunt Sarah's house."

Timothy was still stunned. "Baby, I thought you were in Harrisburg. How did you get to Allentown?"

Reluctantly Teresa confessed, "Daddy... I ran away."

Timothy's car weaved and vibrated as he ran over the rumble strips on the road. He guided the car back onto his lane. "You what!"

Teresa continued with a hint of trepidation in her voice. "Daddy don't be mad. I just couldn't take it anymore."

"But didn't you know I was on my way? I mean this doesn't make any sense. Does your mother know you ran away?"

"Well," Teresa said shyly. "I guess she knows... now."

"Look, I'm approaching Interstate 78 and I'll be there soon, and you better have a good explanation, young lady."

Timothy approached the street where he lived and was quite upset that he had to park a block and a half away. He passed several row houses in route to his home. He began to ponder again whether or not his beloved uncle could be Yahweh's True Psalmist. While Bishop Graystien was not judgmental, he was extremely serious about worship. He was also disapproving of some of the lifestyles of the Gospel artists. Without a doubt, his uncle knew most, if not all of the artists personally. Many, if not all of them had performed at his large church in Philadelphia. Timothy further reasoned that his uncle would no doubt have access to the artists' personal contact information. His uncle was also one of the few people that knew Zachariah Phillips had contacted him.

Timothy shook his head from side to side to indicate his conclusion that it would be impossible for his uncle to be a part of this whole True Psalmist affair. As he approached his steps, he could see his aunt and his daughter peering out the living room window.

His aunt opened the door, pulled him toward her and whispered, "Now Tim, don't be too rough on her. She's been crying almost the entire time she's been here."

"Alright Auntie, I'll be gentle."

Aunt Sarah smile. "Thanks, Tim."

Teresa approached her father with a shy, yet guilty expression on her face. "Hi Dad." She managed to say. "Are we leaving soon to see Pos-I-tive Rhema?"

Timothy refrained himself from being harsh and gently replied, "I think we need to talk first. How did you get here?" He then led her into the living room and they both sat on Aunt Sarah's well-worn love seat.

With some pride she announced, "I caught the bus all by myself. You see, I've been saving up my allowance."

"Well then," Timothy wondered. "Why couldn't you wait for me to pick you up?"

"Dad," she appealed. "I couldn't wait another minute in that place. You see, I've been catching hell at that house."

"Watch your tongue, young lady." He instructed her.

"Now Daddy," she insisted, "you tell me what it is. What is it when you're treated like a second-class person? What do you call the place where you're merely like Cinderella being mistreated by her evil stepsisters and stepmother? I couldn't sleep at night worrying whether or not something would happen to me. I was even having nightmares."

"Was it really that bad?" Timothy countered. "It couldn't have been that bad. Now come on, girl. Did anyone touch you? Did they physically abuse you?"

"Daddy listen to me. Someone doesn't have to touch you to abuse you. Can't you understand that?" Teresa was trying to get her father to see things in a different perspective.

"They left me alone in the house while they were at an all-night revival at the church. They took the baby with them. I'm tired of being left alone while they go off to church and eat at Cracker Barrel. So, I got on a bus and here I am. Daddy, I'm not going back there. If I can't stay with you, I'll stay with Aunt Sarah. Or I'll stay with Karen. I'll stay anywhere, but there. I mean it, Daddy. I'm for real."

Timothy asked, "Has your mother tried to contact you? Does she know where you are?

Teresa advised him. "I left a note for her. I also texted her. Then I left a voice mail."

Timothy inquired, "Do you mean to tell me that she hasn't contacted you at all since you left? How long have you been here?"

Teresa replied, "I got here this afternoon, a little while before you arrived. Aunt Sarah just called Mommy just before you came and told her that I was here and that I was okay. Mommy told Aunt Sarah since I thought I was grown; I should live with my Daddy. Therefore, here I am. I'm staying here with you and Auntie. Aunt Sarah even has a little fold up bed for me, or I can sleep on the couch in your apartment. It's nicer and much better than the bed that I had in hades. See Dad, I didn't say 'hell' "

Timothy smirked and extended his hand. "If you're going to Brooklyn with me, you'd better get your suitcase and a jacket in case it gets chilly." Timothy winked at Aunt Sarah and said, "We'll catch you later. My daughter's coming with me."

Chapter 10

"The Heart Of A Child"

"WITHHOLD NOT CORRECTION FROM THE CHILD:
FOR IF THOU BEATEST HIM WITH THE ROD, HE SHALL NOT DIE"
PROVERBS 23:13

Teresa placed her phone in her lap and announced, "Dad, Karen's on the phone. She wants to talk to you. Would you like for me to put the speaker on? You know it's not safe to hold the phone while you're driving."

Timothy turned the music down on the radio and agreed, "Yeah, you can put the speaker on." He didn't know what he was going to hear from Karen, but he felt that she wouldn't fuss too much at him with his daughter listening to their conversation.

Karen's voice emphasized concern. "Timothy, can you hear me?"

There were a few moments of silence because Timothy thought she might had been upset with him because he hadn't contacted her in weeks. Teresa finally broke the silence, "We can hear you. Daddy, aren't you going to say something?"

He briefly glanced at the phone and replied, "Yeah, I can hear you Karen. You sound upset. What's up?" He hadn't contacted her for during his bout with drugs, and it could be quite reasonable for her to be thoroughly perturbed with this behavior.

During their last encounter, he was aggressively pursuing a more physical intimate interaction, while she was hoping that marriage would be the intimate goal within their grasps. She quoted Scriptures to convince him of the importance of avoiding marriage before sex. He quoted lyrics from love songs. Her logical approach of interpretation of Scriptures ultimately defeated his aggressiveness. She would push him away and declare, "My Bible tells me that '*It is better to marry than to burn*'. I love you Tim, but I can't go to judgment and hell for you." He felt defeated and rejected and Timothy recalled their last encounter when he stormed out the house. He then began to ignore all the important things in his life, including Karen, her son, his business, and especially his daughter. This in turn, was the beginning him latching on to what he assumed was his brief affair with narcotics. His mind was trying to convince him that he conquered his addiction, but his body often urged him to take another trip.

In a business-like tone, he asked, "How can I help you?" He felt foolish at his choice of words. "I mean what can I do for you?" He felt even more embarrassed.

Karen cautioned, "Timothy Samuels, perhaps you need to pull over so we can talk privately and not on this speaker."

Timothy's concern increased as he acknowledges her request and then replied, "I'll pull over at Burger King. It's a few miles away. Teresa can go inside and get a Whopper meal and get me a Doctor Pepper." Timothy drove seven miles and then pulled into the parking lot. "It's okay Karen. Teresa's ordering her food."

"Timothy, "she began to express. "I know we've had our disagreements and all that."

He made a sincere effort to respond with some degree of empathy. "Yes Karen, you are so right. It's all my fault. I was just being selfish. I apologize."

Before he could utter another syllable, she quipped, "I don't have much time before Teresa gets back. This is not about you or me. It's about the children. Do you understand what I mean? It's about your daughter, and my son, Johnnie. Can you get that through your head? There could actually be some kind of an attack on our children. I know you've heard from   the Emperor of Gospel Music. And there's also rumors about something that happened to Archduke Joktan. I can't take any chances with my child. Hey, is Karen still in the restaurant?"

Timothy replied, "Yes, there's a few people in front of her."

"Well," Karen continued. "I know that you heard of the True Psalmist. You're going to be at the G-POW Convention as a blogger-photographer. I received a text from this character who called himself, Son of Yahweh's True Psalmist."

Without hesitation, he informed her, "I received something from him too. Something about *'departing from evil'*. I was hired by Zachariah Phillips to see what I could dig up on this Yahweh's True Psalmist guy. Don't let it upset you so much. Tell me what's happening? Don't keep me in suspense. What did it say? Hurry up, they're waiting on her now."

Karen proceeded, "Timothy here's what he texted me: *'Withhold not correction from the child: for if thou beatest him with the rod, he shall not die.'* You see, this is not about us anymore, it's about my son, and maybe even your girl." She sighed heavily and then asked, "Do you understand? It's like he wants me to beat my child. My child has autism, and even if he didn't, I could never beat him. Can you tell me what this all means?"

Timothy's throat was almost desert dry as he managed to talk in low tones. "Karen, she's on her way to the car, I will call you when we get to the hotel in Jersey City, okay?"

Karen acknowledged, "Sure Timothy. Call me when you get a private moment." Timothy exited the car with the phone in one hand and opened the door for Teresa with the other. "One more thing, Tim. I still love you, though I may not understand why. Bye."

Timothy smiled at his daughter to camouflage any concern as she entered the car. "I know, Karen. I understand and I care, I'm on it. I'll call you later, bye." He couldn't pull himself to use the *love* word, but he wanted her to know that regarding this particular incidence, he cared not only for her, but for the two children.

As Karen munched on her burger, she inquired, "Dad, are you and Karen still going all lovey-dovey?"

Timothy feigned a little smile and replied, "Something like that. Now, don't spill any ketchup on these seats. This is not my car; they're just letting me use it until after the Convention." They both grinned as Teresa set up her phone to play through the car's sound system.

"Check this out Dad," Teresa suggested. "Since we're going to see Pos-I-tive Rhema, let's check out some of his recent stuff. I think he's really cool. He's one of my favorites."

Timothy nodded in agreement. *'Perhaps,'* he thought. *'Some music might keep my mind off of what Karen was talking about.'* "Sure," he said. "I really don't like hip-hop music, maybe you can get me to see things your way. Maybe, these hip-hop tunes could be the key to converting me, but I doubt it."

Teresa said, "Just listen, this is one of his biggest hits. It's called *'The Wall'*."

Timothy wondered out loud, "'The Wall? Michael Jackson had an album called '*Off the Wall*', and a group called Pink Floyd and Bruce Springsteen had songs about '*The Wall*'.'" He was intrigued by the music as it boomed throughout the car. "I hear samplings from Mozart, Thelonious Monk, Duke Ellington, and even a hint of 1950's doo-wop. It was amazing how the artist used such a wide range of classifications of music and unite them all together with afro-centric rhythms. It's an amazing and well-polished sound."

Teresa suggested, "Dad, can you stop going all Old-School music historian on me, and just listen to this?" Teresa began to sway from side to side as the music boomed from the loudspeakers.

Timothy liked the musical arrangements but tried to hide his disapproval of the lyrics. "Are you sure this is Gospel music, baby? I hear some strange words. Would you mind turning it down a little. To be honest with you, I really need to talk to this guy. This music sounds well-polished, but those words seem too inappropriate for Gospel music."

"Inappropriate?" Teresa queried. "Now Dad, when did you become so deep? It's just a song. I know you heard these words before."

"Maybe I did hear some of these words before," he told her. "But I don't think I've ever heard them in church."

73

The car entered the Route 440 East toward the Verrazano-Narrows Bridge. Timothy was terrified going over the bridge. He took a deep breath, held the steering wheel ever-so-tightly, keeping his eyes straight ahead. He couldn't let his daughter know how much he feared crossing bridges, and this bridge in particular. He turned the radio completely off, did not communicate with his daughter and began sweating profusely. Teresa could sense his tension and obvious fear as they maneuvered over the long expanse of the bridge. She would not reveal to him that she was aware of his apparent displeasure and uneasiness regarding the bridge. She focused her attention on the crystal-clear blue water and was excited when Coney Island came into view. Timothy was equally excited because he was finally getting off the bridge.

There were at least three or four bridges that went into Brooklyn. He wondered why his GPS instructed him to go over this particular bridge. He would have felt much safer going over the Manhattan, Williamsburg, or the Brooklyn Bridge with their strongly woven cables. The old bridges would have been a longer route and would have taken him through the crowded streets of Manhattan. The long aesthetically beautiful Verrazano-Narrows bridge didn't seem as safe and secure as the other older bridges. He got a reprieve to relax when he exited the dreaded bridge and followed the signs to I-278. He obeyed the mechanical voice of the GPS as it guided him to the 7th Avenue and the John Cortesse Way exit, and on to Pos-I-tive Rhema's brown stone apartment in Park Slope. He mumbled to himself as they exited the car. "I'm not ever taking this route again. I'll set the GPS for Manhattan via the Manhattan Bridge, and then on to Jersey City by the Holland Tunnel."

As they climbed the stairs, Teresa asked, "Daddy, did you say something?"

"No baby, I was just talking to myself."

Chapter 11

"Don't Touch What
You Don't Understand"

"SAYING TOUCH NOT MY ANOINTED,
AND DO MY PROPHET NO HARM"
PSALM 105:15

Pos-I-tive Rhema's maid immediately answered the doorbell and escorted Timothy and Teresa to the sunken living room. The maid announced, "Mr. and Mrs. Widbell will be with you in a few moments. Make yourself comfortable. We've prepared some refreshments for you."

As the maid exited, Teresa relaxed in the luxuriously appointed leather chaise lounge chair. "Dad," she said trying to hold back her excitement. "I didn't know he was married. I didn't even know his real name. Oh man, this chair is so smooth and soft. Was that his mother who answered the door?"

Timothy informed her, "I seriously doubt that his mother would call him and his wife, 'Mister and Misses Widbell. I think it might be his maid."

With enthusiasm she exclaimed, "Wow! He must be really rich. He has his own maid."

Timothy hinted, "Well, there must be some good money in this Gospel Music racket."

Timothy and his daughter were somewhat startled as Pos-I-tive Rhema and his wife entered the room without making an audible sound. "Hello, Mr. Samuels," Pos-I-tive Rhema said. "I would like you to meet my wife, Mrs. Gynifer Widbell. Before we have you come into our dining room, I'd like to segue to the statement you recently made regarding Gospel music being a so-called racket."

Timothy tried to explain his poor choice of words. "I didn't mean any offence, Mr. Pos-I-tive Rhema."

Pos-I-tive Rhema smiled, and quipped, "If you prefer, you can call me by my birth name, Jacob. As to my success, it has more to do with being fortuitous with the Lord's blessings than what you consider a Gospel music racket." He extended his hand to Teresa, grinned and said, "You must be Teresa. Your father has been blessed with a child of such opulent qualities." Teresa blushed and flashed a smile revealing all her teeth.

Gynifer glanced at her husband and suggested, "Let's feed our guest. They must be famished after that long trip from Pennsylvania. We can discuss this later. Mr. Samuels and Miss Teresa, follow me to the dining room."

Pos-I-tive Rhema agreed, "Yes, I praise Yahweh for my prudent and assiduous wife."

Timothy took a mental note of his use of the Name, Yahweh. As Timothy and Teresa followed the two into the immense dining room, Timothy whispered into her ear. "He sure doesn't talk like this on his records."

Teresa asked in ever so soft tone, "Are you sure we're at the right address? He kind of looks like him in the videos and pictures, but he looks a lot different in person." Timothy gave her a glance to indicate that they should remain silent and discuss this later.

As the maid served the food, Gynifer explained, "People don't know or understand my husband's ministry. We heard you refer to his ministry as a racket of some sorts. Let me explain. We both come from extremely wealthy families. All of the money from his albums, downloads, and concerts are earmarked for various charities."

Timothy was astonished to hear this. "So, you're telling us that he makes no money from his music?"

Pos-I-tive Rhema confirmed, "That is correct. I only live on my inheritance, stocks, bonds, annuities, and prudent investments."

Teresa couldn't contain her excitement as she blurted, "Wow. I never knew that."

Pos-I-tive Rhema cautioned, "Please don't release this information regarding our philanthropic and altruistic endeavors to the general public on your blog. My musical ministry image is important, but my image to my Savior is more important. The Scripture proclaims that we should not let our left hand know what our right hand is doing when it comes to charitable giving. Perhaps, you can inspire some of the younger people, by telling them the fact that people are more complicated than the outer shell or outer man displays. I'm quite concerned about my inner man more than how I may appear on the outside. Now, Teresa, let's talk about you. How are you doing in school?"

Teresa sheepishly replied, "School is out now for Summer vacation. I'm doing okay, I guess."

Pos-I-tive Rhema pointed out, "Your education is extremely important to your dad, and most definitely more important to you and your future. Most people don't know that I have a doctorate degree in music from the Julliard School of Music. I am also writing my thesis for my Doctor of Theology Degree from Princeton Theological Seminary. That information should prove to be more beneficial to my younger concert attendees."

Timothy agreed, "That's fascinating. I won't divulge the information regarding your out-reach ministry, though it is quite interesting. I'm sure the younger people would benefit from your educational pursuits. I listened to some of your music on the way here and I found your music to be very intriguing. It was amazing how you blended some many types of music in one song. Your music clearly demonstrates your training in a prestigious school such as Julliard. However, I do have a few questions and concerns regarding the lyrics in your music."

Pos-I-tive Rhema grinned and said, "You may proceed with the inquires, I can defend every lyric and even every syllable in my songs."

"Well then," Timothy continued. "They appear to be, shall I say, *unchristian-like*."

Pos-I-tive Rhema chuckled. "It might appear that way to you, but to my audience, it emulates a positive and opulent message of hope."

Timothy interjected, "To be frank with you, I'm not sure if I want my daughter listening to that type of music and hearing that type of language. She might as well be listening to regular hip-hop. I see no difference."

In spite of the rebuke by Timothy, Pos-I-tive continued. "Every word that seems to be offensive, deleterious, and haughty to you is rooted and emulated from Scripture."

Timothy was impressed with Pos-I-tive's use of his vocabulary and calm demeanor. He continued his interrogation by asking, "Would you mind explaining some lyrics from your song *'The Wall'*?"

Teresa tugged on her father's sleeve and said, "Daddy, stop it. That's one of my favorite songs."

Without a moment's hesitation, Timothy declared, "I bet it is."

Pos-I-tive Rhema stated, "First, let me explain the meaning of my pseudonym, or my professional stage name, Pos-I-tive Rhema. In actuality, Pos-I-tive really needs no explanation. The messages found in my music are always positive and never deleterious. The messages are not enigmas or riddles, or mysterious. The only paradox is that you don't know your Bible. The youth hears the words, do the research, and then get blessed by the obvious, but somewhat hidden true message. That which is a paradox or contradictory to you, becomes a wealth of blessings and useful data to those who comprehend what the true Rhema is saying. It doesn't matter what you think you hear in my music, the message is always full of hope for mankind and adulation for my Lord and Savior, Jesus Christ."

Timothy was feeling as though a nap was coming on because he felt that he was about to hear a sermonette. It seemed as though a spirit of sleep usually came upon him during sermons, speeches, and lectures.

Pos-I-tive pointed out, "Now, let me explain the *'Rhema'* part. Rhema is the spoken Word of God. Now the song *Wall* is based on several Biblical incidents. I shall quote from the words of David, the Psalmist, in I Samuel chapter 25 and verse 22. *'So, and more also do God unto the enemies of David, if I leave of all that pertain to him by the morning light any that pisseth against the wall.'* Don't be offended by my use of the words, *pisseth against the wall*. The term is used 8 times in the Bible. Have you got any more questions, Mr. Samuels?"

Timothy had heard enough Bible teaching for the day, he responded, "No, man. I guess I should read my Bible more. I suppose you'll tell me that bastard and whore are just all throughout the Bible as they are in your songs."

Gynifer chimed in, "God is very forgiving, but he does condemn bastards at least twice in the Old Testament, and once in the New. This term refers to the unfaithful to God, and not used for children whose fathers have not step up to their responsibilities."

Pos-I-tive then offered, "And as for the word piss, it's mentioned eight times in my Bible. Let me conclude by telling you that you can find whore sixty-five times in the Old and New Testament. It generally refers to those who seek and follow after other gods. In today's world, these gods might include money, lust of the flesh, positions, and worldly titles. Other seemingly offensive words you may find in my Bible are damn or damnation, which is mentioned 15 times in Scripture. I suppose you would just die if I said, 'hell', which is found in my Bible 54 times. I don't think I need to go on, do I, Mr. Samuels, now do I? None-the-less, I shall devolve a few more incidents of allegorical evidence that will further demonstrate my utmost sincerity to reign in everyone to the fullness of the Gospel of Jesus Christ."

Pos-I-tive Rhema had a treasure chest of Biblical theology that Timothy and Teresa somehow found to be quite stimulating. Pos-I-tive Rhema's delivery of his Scriptural basis for his music held everyone's attention. Some of his long-detailed explanations almost sounded like sermonettes, but Timothy didn't protest. Usually, sermons and sermonettes would lull him into a state of ultra-weariness which ultimately climaxed in sleep.

In spite of all the detailed information he gleamed from Pos-I-tive Rhema, Timothy was still perplexed as he formulated what he wanted to reveal about him in his blog. "No, Mr. Pos-I-tive Rhema, I think you made your point crystal clear. Now, would you mind if I took a few photos for the blog? Also, I have one more question to ask you before we leave. But before I ask this question, I would like to thank you and your wife for your wonderful hospitality. Now, I want to be as frank and honest as possible; and I don't want to offend you. However, I must pursue this inquiry."

Pos-I-tive agreed. "I will give you a complete and non-condescendingly abrupt and truthful evaluation."

Timothy prepared himself to ask the question. He glanced at his daughter, briefly shifted his attention onto Gynifer, and then finally focused his eyes on Pos-I-tive Rhema. "Let me preference the main question, by asking you if you have received any correspondence from the so-called Yahweh's True Psalmist?" He observed as Pos-I-tive shook his head from side to side to indicate a negative response. He was surprised that the seemingly talkative man gave a silent answer. Timothy continued, "Then, let me get directly to the point. Are you Yahweh's True Psalmist?"

Pos-I-tive Rhema looked at his hardwood walnut floor for few moments, lifted his head as stood to his feet, shook Timothy's hand. He then embraced him and replied, "Most indubitably, no, I am not."

As Timothy gathered his equipment and headed toward the car, his mind was full of questions that he should have asked Pos-I-tive Rhema. His instinct told him that his daughter would have even more questions and that she would be bombarding him with some type of cross-examination all the way to their next destination.

The LORD's Song In A Strange Land

Chapter 12

"Speak The Right Thing"

"YEA, MY HEART SHALL REJOICE,
WHEN YOUR LIPS SPEAK RIGHT THINGS" PROVERBS 23:16

To his surprise, Timothy wasn't inundated with questions from his apparently curious daughter. They rode in complete silence until they entered the Holland Tunnel on their way to the Double Tree Hotel in Jersey City. Timothy finally shattered the silence. "Teresa, I know that you must have a ton of questions about Pos-I-tive Rhema. Why are you so quiet now?"

Teresa placed a hand on her cheek as if she was in deep thought and then admitted, "Dad, you know singers and people like that are so different when you see them up close."

Timothy smiled as he asked, "What do you mean by that?" She tapped him on his shoulder and said, "Dad, you know what I mean, don't you?" Before he could respond, she continued. "On his videos he seemed like someone I could relate to. You know, what I mean?"

As the car continued through the tunnel, Timothy replied, "I think so, but why don't you explain it to me."

Teresa then tried to put her thoughts into words. "Dad, I'm not saying he's phony or anything like that. I'm just saying he was using all those big words and stuff. He doesn't use those type words in his videos and songs. He had me kind of confused."

Timothy agreed with her. "He had me sort of confused too. Especially when I asked him about Yahweh's True Psalmist."

Teresa asked her father, "Dad, just what is this Yahweh's True Psalmist? I heard you when you asked Pos-I-tive Rhema about that? It seemed to be so mysterious."

The two remained silent for a while as the car slowly proceeded toward the exit into Jersey City. Timothy monitored the GPS as it guided him toward the hotel. He finally broke the silence. "Regarding this Yahweh's True Psalmist, I suppose that that it's more like a who, rather than a what."

Timothy steered the car toward the exit ramp of the tunnel as he was guided by his GPS to the hotel. Timothy tried to explain. "Well, I suppose it's more like a who, rather than a what, Yahweh's True Psalmist is."

Teresa then responded, "Well okay, then who is he?"

Timothy pointed out, "Nobody knows if he's a he, or a she or maybe both."

Teresa's curiosity was at a peak. "Are you saying this person is like androgynous?"

Timothy quickly quipped, "Where did you learn such a large word. Perhaps from your favorite Gospel hip-hop artist, Pos-I-tive Rhema."

"Oh Daddy," she blurted, "Everybody knows what that is. A person that could be sort of part guy and part girl"

Timothy informed her, "No, baby. I don't know if he or she is androgynous. You see, this may be the work of more than one individual. He's sort of like an enigma wrapped up in an ambivalent package."

Teresa let out a loud laugh as they proceeded toward the hotel. "Dad, now you're talking like Pos-I-tive Rhema. Now, tell me what has this Psalmist person done that's so important? "

Timothy spoke in low tones. "Teresa, let's register, get settled in our room, and then I'll tell you as much as I'm permitted."

They entered the spacious suite and Timothy said, "You can have the large bedroom and I'll camp out here on the couch."

"Okay, Dad. Are you sure you don't want to sleep in this big luxurious room? I don't mind sleeping on the couch."

As Timothy unpacked the luggage he replied, "It's okay. You can have the luxurious and spacious bedroom with the large flat screen. After all, you deserve to have royal treatment, my little princess."

"Oh Daddy, you're the greatest," she exclaimed. Now, can we talk about the Psalmist person? What did he do? Did he or she do something bad? How does he contact people? Did he contact you? Who else did he contact?"

Timothy waved his hands and replied, "Woah girl, slow down. You sound like you're interrogating me."

"I'm sorry, Dad. This sounds so exciting."

Timothy decided to fill her in on some of the details of his assignment. "You see I was hired by Zachariah Phillips to find out about this nuisance."

Teresa's eyes flashed with excitement. "You mean Zachariah Phillips, the Emperor of Gospel music? And working with the other Gospel giant artists? And you are sort of like a detective. Wow! This sounds so exciting

Timothy cautioned her, "This is not a game. Zachariah Phillip's car was shot up. There're rumors that some guy named Archduke Joktan was attacked while he was in a bathtub. Zachariah's son's car was damaged too."

Teresa interjected, "Dad, this Psalmist person is not playing, is he? This really is so ex--"

88

Timothy interrupted her before she could finish her statement. "Yeah, I know, so exciting. I received a text from this Psalmist and Karen also received one."

Teresa ran toward her father, embraced him and exclaimed, "No, Daddy. Not you, and Karen. Do you think he wants to harm you, Karen, and especially, Little Johnnie?"

Timothy hunched his shoulders. "I don't know. Maybe because her son, Johnnie is attending the G-POW convention. Maybe this Psalmist is a performer. Maybe this person is jealous of the other performers. I don't know. I'll find out and try to stop him before he does any more harm."

Teresa nervously asked, "Dad is there a place around here to get something to eat? I'm kind of hungry."

Timothy was totally flabbergasted. "Are you kidding me? I thought you wanted to hear about my assignment and Yahweh's True Psalmist."

Teresa rubbed her stomach and said, "Dad when I get nervous, I get hungry. I'm nervous about what this guy or girl or whatever might hurt little Johnnie Roberts. And if you and Karen ever get married, he might be my little brother. I'm really nervous. Let's go to the White Castle. Didn't we pass one on the way here?"

At first Timothy was not in the mood or state of mind to leave the comfort of the hotel suite. He realized his own comforts were superseded by his daughter's uneasiness. He also realized that his daughter's concern for Johnnie was sincere. The two children had been friends since he became involved with Karen, Johnnie's mother. Johnnie had few if any friends or acquaintances. Johnnie's autism often precluded him from being too involved with other children, as well as adults. However, Johnnie Roberts was known throughout the Gospel music world as a genuine prodigy.

Timothy headed towards the door and acquiesced to his daughter's request. "Okay, Princess Teresa," he teasingly said as he bowed and extended his hand. "Your wish is granted. I think I remember passing a White Castle on J.F.K. Boulevard."

As they proceeded to enter the car Teresa insisted, "Dad, please don't play any music."

As Timothy started the car he asked, "Why? I thought that you enjoyed listening to our music." The two traveled in silenced as the car headed in the direction of John Fitzgerald Kennedy Boulevard. Timothy patted his daughter's hand. "Listen Teresa, are you really upset about Karen and I being contacted by the Psalmist?"

Teresa tried to hide her concerns with a slight smile. "Daddy, I'm most concerned about Johnnie and what might happen to him. After all, some terrible things happened to the other people. Johnnie is so innocent. Daddy, why are people so jealous of others? Didn't God give Johnnie his gift of music? He's incredibly special to me. Isn't he special to you, Dad?"

Timothy responded as earnestly as he could as he parked the car. "Yes, you should know that by now."

"I mean Daddy, when was the last time that you actually talked with him?"

Timothy shut the motor to the car off. "Now, you know that I've always talked with him. Sometimes he just says the same thing over and over. It's like he's not paying any attention to me."

Teresa gently pushed her father's hand away as she chided him. "You and Karen have been going out for a long time and you should know that autistic children often talk like that. It's called scripting. He merely repeats lyrics to songs, things he heard his mother say, and bits from sermons that he's heard. I mean, when was the last time that you tried to have a conversation with him? I have conversations with him all the time. His speech therapist, Ms. Joneson has worked wonders with him, just in the past few months. I suppose you were too wrapped up in your own little problems to deal with me, or Karen, or little Johnnie."

Timothy felt quite embarrassed to admit that he hadn't really had a conversation with too many people lately. He was too occupied entertaining himself with his own pity party and his bouts with OxyContin. He was only able to respond to his daughter by asking, "What would you like to eat?"

She continued chiding him, "I suppose you were so caught up in your own little situations that you couldn't deal with anybody else's problems. By the way, I think I'll have 3 fish filets, some french fries, three cheeseburgers with extra pickles, some onion rings, and a large orange soda."

The two exited the card and headed toward the entrance of the restaurant. Timothy sighed loudly and responded, "You certainly must be really, really, truly upset."

Chapter 13

"Too Sick To Feel The Pain"

"THEY HAVE STRICKEN ME, SHALT THOU SAY, AND I WAS NOT SICK,
THEY HAVE BEATEN ME, AND I FELT IT NOT:"
PROVERBS 23:35A

"OOOOH Daddy," Teresa grunted trying to get the attention of her father who was soundly asleep on the couch. Her moans could not penetrate the closed door or the booming snoring emanating from her exhausted father. She was entirely too weak to raise herself from the bed, and definitely could not walk the short distance to get her father's attention. Consequently, she continued to moan, rub her stomach, and roll back and forth in her bed in anguish. She reached over to the night table, picked her phone up, and dialed her father's number. Timothy was wrapped up in deep sleep and couldn't hear the phone as it vibrated and rang out the ring tone he had assigned for his daughter.

Teresa, bent over with pain, took great effort, got out of bed, opened the door, and called out again to her father. "Daddy, wake up!" She shuffled over to him, shook him gently and called out, "Daddy, wake up. Please. My stomach."

The desperate pleas from his daughter and her constantly gently shaking him, startled him out of dreamland. He

93

suddenly sat up, pivoted to face her and rubbed his eyes, "Girl, what's up? What's happening?"

Teresa moaned as she indicated, "Daddy, I'm so sick. My stomach's been turning all night."

With the least bit of sympathy, Timothy coldly responded, "What did you expect, honey? I mean all that greasy food before going to sleep doesn't let anyone sleep well at night."

Contradicting her father, she retorted, "Daddy, please don't make me laugh. You ate just as much as I did, and I almost had to light a firecracker to wake you up." They both managed to laugh. "I'm serious, my stomach is really killing me."

"Alright, I'll go downstairs and see if there's some Alka-Seltzer or Tums downstairs."

Teresa let out a moan, "No, Daddy. Please don't leave me here all by myself."

Timothy took her by the hand, gently pinched her cheek, and assured her, "You're a big girl now. I'll only be gone for a few minutes. I tell you what, I'll go down the hallway near the vending machines and get you a Pepsi or a Coke that should settle your stomach a little."

She sat next to her father, nodding her head in affirmation. "Dad, don't you think a ginger ale might be better. If they don't have ginger ale, the colas should do the trick."

He slipped his bathrobe on and headed out the door. He returned with a bucket of ice and a bottle of Pepsi Cola. "Here," he said as he poured the soda into a cup and added some ice. "This should make you feel better. Now, don't drink it too quickly."

"Okay, Dad."

"Did you know that Pepsi was originally made for dyspepsia?"

He knew that this question would arouse her curiosity. "Dad, are you serious? Pepsi is just a soda, that's all."

"You're right. Now it's just a soda, but when it was invented, it was made for upset stomachs, which was called dyspepsia, that's where they got the name Pepsi. Are you feeling any better? By the way, what time is it?"

She glanced at his cell phone, "I feel a little better. It's almost nine o'clock. Hey Dad, someone's trying to reach you. Your phone's ringing, and I can see it's Zachariah Phillips."

She handed the phone to her dad. "Hello, Mr. Phillips. How may I help you?"

The Emperor of Gospel Music inquired, "How did the meeting with Pos-I-tive Rhema go?"

Timothy whispered to Teresa, "Go, take a shower and get dressed while I talk with Mr. Phillips." Teresa smiled and made her way back to her room. He continued his talk with Mr. Phillips, "It went well. He's quite a character. You know, I asked him bluntly whether or not he was Yahweh's True Psalmist."

Zachariah Phillips' held his anger back and asked, "And you expected him to give you an honest answer? Are you serious? I'm starting to doubt why I even hired you."

Timothy felt the need to defend himself. "Hey, if you want me off the case, it's cool. I mean man, it's real cool. Let me tell you how I feel about this whole situation."

"I'm listening, go ahead."

"I also received some contact from this Psalmist dude and my girlfriend feels threatened by his texts. So, if you want to relieve me, it's alright. I'll stay on this case on my own, because now it's personal. I felt that I could feel Pos-I-tive Rhema out. In my honest professional opinion, who really knows what or who this guy is. We don't know his motivation, or even if it's a group conspiracy. God only knows."

Zachariah Phillips apologetically conceded, "Wait a minute, Tim. Perhaps I was a little hasty. We're all kind of tensed up. I suppose we can both agree that the investigation should continue."

"Listen Mr. Phillips, I don't want my daughter to hear us conversing about this stuff. She's concerned about Little Johnnie Roberts whose mother received a threatening text. Let's continue this conversation later. I'm heading for Gary Indiana to check out the praise dancers that you emailed me about."

Zachariah Phillips chuckled a little, "Okay Timothy, keep me posted regarding what's going on. I apologize for---"

"No problem," Timothy interjected. "Bye." A few minutes later he heard the doorknob turn as Teresa entered the room. "Are you feeling any better, baby?" He asked.

Feigning a smile, she responded, "Yes, a little better. I think the Pepsi did the trick for me. How are you feeling, Dad?"

He rose to his feet, stretched and replied, "I'm fine. I'm going to take a shower and get ready to go to Gary, Indiana. Would you like to come with me or stay with your Aunt Sarah?" Without a moment's hesitation, she purred, "I'm going with you."

"Solid, Teresa. We'll have to go to Boscov's to get you some more clothes. Now listen, try not to get upset again, alright. When you get upset, you eat a lot of crazy stuff, and then you get sick. So, try not to get upset, understand?"

"Sure, Dad. Everything's cool now."

Chapter 14

"Disorder My Steps"

"ORDER MY STEPS IN THY WORD: AND LET NOT ANY INIQUITY HAVE DOMINION OVER ME." PSALM 119:133

Ceremonious is the only professional liturgical dance troupe that will attend the G-POW convention. Their dance performance will be the zenith of the praise dance portion of the convention. Their dynamic, athletic performances have set the entire Gospel music industry in a tailspin. The older traditional church goers were vehemently opposed to their dance performances. Many of these traditional church goers feel that dances should not be rehearsed but should be under the unction of the Holy Spirit. In fact, that's precisely why they condemned their dance routines.   The so-called 'Seasoned Saints' and the more traditional younger people never considered their dance movements as a 'praise dance', but merely a secular performance. That's the word that was used all the time, it's just a *performance*. Their popularity was increasing by leaps and bounds due to the total hypnotic movements that were sometimes deemed too sensual. Not surprisingly, there has been an exponential increase of men flocking to their seductive performances.

Ceremonious contacted Zachariah Phillips with an urgent request for him to come to Gary, Indiana.   They had informed him that they had received a cryptic message from

Yahweh's True Psalmist, which they promptly forwarded to Zachariah Phillips who then sent it to Timothy.

Timothy utilized YouTube to view some of their performances in order for him to be more prepared for his initial contact with them. He decided to view their performances in chronological order to see how the group evolved over time. He invited his daughter to help him critique and understand the whole liturgical-praise dance phenomenon.

"Wow Dad," Teresa exclaimed. "These girls are awesome. I love them. Did you see their dancewear? This is awesome. I want to praise dance at Uncle Graystien's church. They are such an inspiration."

Timothy admitted, "Yeah, they seemed to be fairly good. Let's check out some more recent stuff." The two viewed several more performances and Timothy began to notice a pattern. "Terry, these dances seem more appropriate for the club. I mean girl, this is getting more and more crazy. I'm not too sure I want you doing these types of dances. The first couple of dances were pretty nice, but these more recent ones are a little risqué." He exited YouTube and declared, "We'd better get a move on if we're going to get to Gary anytime soon."

Teresa disapprovingly, "Aww Dad, it was just getting good."

The two gathered their belongings and checked out of the hotel.

Ceremonious began their rehearsal and planning session in the basement of the Moment of Joyful Praise Church to plan for the upcoming G-POW convention.

The four members of the exclusive group held hands, closed their eyes, and nodded in agreement as the founder and choreographer, Myra-Ann began the prayer. "Heavenly Father, we beseech you to hear our prayer. We want to praise you with the sincerity of David when he danced before You with all his might. We strive to dance like David when he danced out of his clothes and put on the priest's linen ephod. Amen"

The three other dancers, Florance, Hazela and Karoln echoed "Amen."

The ladies sat in a circle with their legs in a '*crisscross applesauce*' fashion. Myra-Ann explained that she used the crisscross applesauce term ever since she learned that expression from her first dance instructor while she was in pre-school.

Florance decided to commence the discussion with the message sent by the Son of Yahweh's Psalmist. "Girls, this text has me really upset. I mean why would we receive this mess? What have we done other than to try to praise the Lord with our sincere dances?"

Hazela chastised, "Now Flo, you know there is some controversy about our most recent dances."

Myra-Ann showed her discontent for Hazela's remark with chastisement. "Florance, how dare you question the goodness of the Lord. We are the highest paid praise dancers on the planet. In fact, I can't think of any group of praise dancers that come anywhere near our class with success."

Karoln, who is usually the quieter and reflective of the group, insisted. "Girls, we have to admit that our success has been great. Is it really that important to our ministry? I mean aren't we supposed to be a minis--"

Myra-Ann quickly halted her in mid-sentence. "Were you going to say ministry? Now, don't tell me the silent one is now complaining. Before I organized this dance troupe, you were all living with your parents and working an occasional temporary job at various Amazon warehouses and at Walmart. You spent more time unemployed than you did working. You shouldn't be such an ingrate."

Karoln reverted back to her customary silent state and wouldn't offer a defense. Hazela didn't hesitate to rationalize for her friend, Karoln. "Now Myra-Ann Jenkins, let's be for real. Our dances have sort of glided into the worldly realm."

Myra-Ann retaliated, "I suppose Karoln, you're not happy with your new car, new apartment, and the success we have attained. All of our future performances are literally sold out."

Hazela shyly inserted, "Our performances may be selling out, but are we selling out on the Lord and to the enemy."

Myra-Ann rose to her feet, glaring at the ladies. "Well, I suppose I may have to get some new dancers. Ya'll know people are knocking down the doors to get into this elite group. Well, speak up. If you don't like the way things are going, you can just leave now. You're not irreplaceable. In fact, for our upcoming shows, I'm hiring some male dancers."

Karoln protested, "Are you serious, Myra-Ann? Folks are already saying that some of our dances are a bit too sexy. What are they going to say if we include some men to our routine?"

Myra-Ann paced around the large room several times, her fists were clenched, and her facial expression indicated precisely how she felt.

She took a deep breath and then uttered, "Like I said, if you don't want to be in this group, just leave. I don't need any of you, understand? I don't need negative people around me. I mean to take this group to higher heights, understand?"

The other three ladies had the same thought: *'Are we going on to higher heights or slipping into lower depths?'*

Karoln cautioned, "Now ladies, let's just discuss the business at hand. Come on Myra-Ann, sit down and let's deal with our new dance apparel. We can also discuss the new dances. Can we all agree on that, girls? We can deal with the new male members later. We don't have much time. We must make a good impression at the convention in order for us to maintain our position." The ladies nodded in agreement.

Myra-Ann slowly glided back down to the floor and resumed her previous sitting position. She gradually smiled, inwardly she knew that she had the group in the palm of her hand. "Thanks, girls. When Timothy Samuels arrives, we'll deal with the Yahweh's True Psalmist situation. Our new dance interpretations will consist of music without lyrics."

Florance could not resist the urge to chime in. "You mean that we will be dancing to praise music without words?"

Myra-Ann smirked. "That's what without lyrics means – no words in the songs, just music."

Hazela blurted, "Our dances are supposed to interpret the words to the songs and move the people, right, ladies?"

Before anyone could support her with an opinion, Myra-Ann challenged her. "Haven't you noticed that often times when people are praise dancing, some people are just listening to the music and lyrics with their eyes closed? With no words

103

to meditate on, everyone's focus will be on us. Now, I have even more great news for us."

"Oh brother," Hazela whispered inaudibly.

Myra-Ann continued, "I had one of my friends design us new liturgical dancewear." She opened a large envelope and handed each of the ladies a detailed drawing of the new dance apparel for the upcoming performances. The other three ladies gasped in disapproval simultaneously but did not have the courage to utter a word.

Chapter 15

"A Fun Dance...A Bun Dance... A Done Dance"

"THEIR LAND BROUGHT FORTH FROGS IN ABUNDANCE, IN THE CHAMBERS OF THEIR KINGS." PSALM 105:30

Teresa firmly protested when Timothy flatly refused to take her to Gary, Indiana to see Ceremonious. "But Daddy," she moaned. "You said I could go. You promised me. How can you break your promise? Where am I going to stay? I'm not going back home with Mama."

Timothy tried to express some tenderness as he guided the car onto the Interstate 95 entrance leading toward Philadelphia. "You don't ever have to worry about going to your mom. You see, I promised Karen that I would see her regarding the convention. You know how she was concerned about Johnnie."

Teresa beamed with anticipation. "Do you mean I'm spending some time with Karen and Johnnie? Oh Daddy, you're the best."

Timothy was becoming gratified that she didn't mind spending some time with Karen. He rationalized that Ceremonious' gradual progression into what he considered inappropriate attire and dance movements, would have an unacceptable influence on his daughter.

The two made small talk until they arrived at Karen's apartment. Excitedly Teresa exited the car, ran up the stairs, and rang the bell several times. When Karen arrived to open the door, she immediately grinned and gave her an ever so tight hug.

"My, my," Karen beamed. "Girl, you almost knocked me down. And you sure have grown."

Teresa scanned the living room as she entered and asked, "Where is Johnnie?"

"Now Terry, aren't you going to at least speak to me? You'd better get on out there and help your dad with your bags."

Timothy had already removed the luggage and remarked, "It's cool, I don't need any help. You go on in and see Johnnie." Timothy entered the room, dropped his load on the floor and embraced Karen. His eyes seemed to have a slight twinkle as he whispered in Karen's ear. "I missed you, baby."

"I missed you too. Now, come on in and let's talk about this Psalmist situation."

The two entered the living room as Karen asked, "Would you like something to eat or drink?"

"No Karen, I'm good." He was slightly nervous, perhaps from the guilt that he felt. The guilt brought on because he hadn't seen her in such a long time. "We can discuss this Psalmist thing for a little while and then I will have to leave. I'm afraid that I can't stay too long. I have to go to Gary, Indiana to see some praise dancers named Ceremonious."

She immediately released his hand upon hearing what he had just said. "Praise dancers? Praise dancers? I know you're not talking about those hoochie mamas! I tell you what. Since those dancers are more important than me and my child, why don't you just leave now."

As she rose to her feet, Timothy tugged on her arm. "Ain't I here for you now? I mean I'm here right now, aren't I? Ceremonious can wait until I get there."

She snatched his hand away and quipped, "Yeah, you're physically here now, but I can guarantee your mind is on those wild wicked women."

Timothy protested, "Baby, it's not at all like that. They're terrified because they received a message from— "

"From the same person or thing that has me and my child all jittery. Tim look, you've got a long way to go in our relationship. And you've got a long way to go to get to Indiana. So, why don't you go. Just leave, I don't want to get all loud right now with the kids in the next room."

Reluctantly Timothy stimulated a smile and slowly exited the apartment. His mind was spinning in circles. He felt that he needed to escape into another world. He contemplated going into his stash of OxyContin that was still nestled safely in his camera bag. *'I just don't understand women,"* he thought. *"Especially church women.'*

Timothy listened to the B.B. King Blues channel on his satellite radio as the GPS guided the car down I-76 toward Harrisburg. He was impressed especially by two of B.B. King's most popular songs. He felt that the blues was apropos for the way he was feeling regarding his relationship with Karen. The tune, *'The Thrill Is Gone'* might as well be his theme song regarding her. He chuckled to himself as B.B. King's lyrics to *'How Blue Can You Get?'* boomed through his speakers. He let out a loud guffaw as his favorite lyrics stated:

'I bought you a brand-new Ford – You said, 'I want a Cadillac'. I bought you a 10-dollar dinner- You said, 'Thanks for the snack' I brought you a penthouse -You said, 'It's just a shack'. I gave you seven children -And now you want to give them back!'

His self-doubt, shame and anger, and the blues coming from his radio, was all he needed for motivation to keep him alert during the 700-mile trip to Indiana. Ten hours later Timothy checked into the hotel. He was mentally and physically drained as he reclined onto the bed and immediately fell into a deep almost hypnotic-like sleep.

The next morning, he was showered, shaved and ready to make some phone calls. He was disheartened that Karen refused to respond to his texts and voice mails. He contacted Ceremonious to make them aware that he would be there within the hour. He also contacted Zachariah Phillips. "Hello, Mr. Phillips. How are things going for you?"

Zachariah, the Emperor of Gospel music, covered his mouth as he coughed. "Well, good morning, Timothy. Great to hear from you. Let me apologize regarding our last conversation."

"No problem," Timothy pointed out. "It's all good, I'm on my way to see Ceremonious. I just drove in from Philly"

"Great, Tim. Listen up, man. I'm forwarding you an American Express card. I would rather you fly to cover more of the artists in a timely fashion. The convention is in a few days. I will Fed-Ex the card to you. Where are you staying now?"

"I'm at the Best Western North West in Hammond."

"Fine, it should arrive first thing tomorrow morning. You can use it for all expenses. Just leave your car at O'Hare and take a flight back to Philly and pick up another car. Listen, I have to go to get things more organized for the upcoming convention. I'll catch you later."

"Solid, Mr. Phillips." They concluded the call and Timothy exited his suite with his camera equipment in tow.

As the GPS led Timothy in circles, Ceremonious involved themselves in mastering the new steps that Myra-Ann had created. Finally, Timothy decided to get directions from a gas station. Unfortunately, the attendant did not understand English. Timothy banged on the dashboard in frustration when he realized that he was on the opposite side of town.

Myra-Ann had completed the dance routine except for the finale. "Girls, you're doing great. Now here's the last part of the dance. Now follow after me, five-six-seven-eight. When the guitar solo hits this note, pivot to the right, with your back to the audience. Then place your hands on your knees. Then do this move for eight counts."

"Wait a minute," Florance protested. "I mean we all went along with you about wearing the skimpy outfits, but this slow-motion twerking is where we have to draw the line. I mean we're hopping and slow-motion twerking like a bunch of frogs in hot water."

Hazel cut in, "Look Florance, what do you mean by *we*? Speak for yourself. I think we can manage this move."

"Yeah, I think it's the best way to conclude the dance and get everyone's attention." Myra-Ann added.

Florance thought, '*Yeah, we're really getting their attention.*'

"Now ladies," Myra-Ann snapped. "We're almost done. Florance, when we turn our backs to the audience, it represents us turning our backs on the world and its pleasures. When we put our hands on our knees, it symbolizes our need to pray. What you consider 'frog- like slow twerking movements, expresses that we're shaking the devil off.'"

The other ladies actually thought her explanation was quite ludicrous, however, Florance was the only one with enough fortitude to protest. Florance, however, not wanting to start another heated discussion, smiled, and stated, "Since you explained it that way, let's get back to work." Inwardly, she knew that this entire dance, the revealing dancewear, and the use of lyric-less music was highly inappropriate. Her thoughts were in conjunction with Hazela and Karoln, but she refused to debate with Myra-Ann – she really needed the money to help support her boyfriend who had just lost his job. Her inner thoughts were: '*How much fun it used to be to dance while praising the Lord. Now it has become a bun dance, with us ladies exposing too much of our backsides.*' She was considering quitting after the convention. She said within herself, '*This use to be a Fun Dance, it has become a show my Bun Dance, and Lord knows it will soon be a Done Dance for me.*' Not only would be a Done Dance for her, if

Yahweh's True Psalmist's plan comes to fruition, Ceremonious will be done, kaput, terminated, and finished.

Chapter 16

"O Daughters Of Gary, Indiana"

"O DAUGHTER OF BABYLON, WHO ART TO BE DESTROYED: HAPPY SHALL HE BE, THAT REWARDETH THEE AS THOU HAS SERVED US."
PSALM 137:8

Wearily Timothy entered the large room and placed his photography equipment on the floor. "Hi, you must be Ceremonious, I'm Timothy Samuels."

Myra-Ann approached Timothy extending her hand. "Hi Timothy, I'm Myra-Ann, the founder and chief choreographer."

Timothy thought, *'Even dancers have to tell you their titles and positions.'* "Pleased to meet you," he said.

"Hey Timothy," Florance said with a smile. "I'm Florance."

"Hi Timothy," Hazela added. "I'm Hezela" pointing, "and this is Karoln."

Myra-Ann bubbled, "We are Ceremonious. You were a little late, but just in time because we just finished our final dance."

Timothy reached into his camera bag, "Is it alright if I take a few still shots, and perhaps a little of the dance for my blog?"

"You're welcome to take as many shots as you like," Myra-Ann informed him. Then she insisted, "We cannot allow you to take any videos of our new dance. The world premiere of the dance will take place during the G-POW convention."

"Well okay," Timothy intoned. He was glad that he hadn't taken his daughter with him. He didn't want her to be influenced by the tight form fitting yoga pants the women were wearing. He pondered, *'How in the world did they get into those pants? Did they spray paint them on? I mean, there's not too much left for an imaginational survey.'* If he had seen their newly planned liturgical dancewear, he would have had a mild stroke. Their new outfits included no leggings, or yoga pants, just skimpy translucent material covering their highly revealing curvaceous and shapely limbs.

Timothy felt somewhat uncomfortable as they all sat down on the floor to discuss the Psalmist situation. His bones were creaking, and he found it difficult to sit with his legs crossed. He extended his legs and leaned back on his arms. "Now can you tell me about the message you received from this character."

Hazela cautioned, "I wouldn't classify this guy as a character. I would say he's sort of a devil or demonic force."

Timothy said, "You may be right, Hazela. We haven't ascertained whether it's a man, a woman, or a group. Can you tell me exactly what you received?"

Myra-Ann reached inside her bra and pulled out a slip of paper and read it out loud: "*Ladies of Lucifer, who is lord of darkness and your master, take note of this warning: 'O daughter of Babylon, who art to be destroyed. Psalm 137:8. Yahweh's True Psalmist'.*"

Timothy's face showed some genuine surprise. "Ladies, I'm not trying to alarm you, but I read several messages from this person, and this is the first one with seems to be an actual threat. I have received a message, Zachariah has received one along with his son, Amoz, and others. Their messages merely quoted Biblical Scriptures. Your message calls you out as ladies of Lucifer. Based on the context of the Scripture, you seemed to be threatened with destruction. You must be aware of the rumor that someone attacked this guy named, Archduke Johtan. Someone attached him while he was taking a bath. I was also wondering why you hadn't locked the door after receiving this threat. I was able to just walk right in here."

Myra-Ann with confidence pointed out, "We're in the safest part of Gary, and we rely on the Lord to protect us."

Florance eyes widened as she gasped. "Perhaps, we'd better keep the door locked from now on. My Lord, I didn't know about any of this stuff. What else has happened?"

Timothy motioned with his hands to ease their concerns. "Now ladies, I don't think anything serious has happened. It

115

seems like it's like bizarre jokes. Do you know why he would consider you aligned with Lucifer or the devil?"

Myra-Ann tried to calm the others in the group. "Now, don't get it twisted, girls. You all know that we are not in league with the devil or demons or any such thing. We serve the Almighty. We should not have the spirit of fear, and we should be of a sound mind."

The other members of the group had basically this same thought: '*Now she's quoting Scriptures. What about where the Bible says our dress should be modest? What about the Scripture that tells us not to be part of the world?*'

Timothy pressed the group. "Is there anything that you may have done, or will be doing that can be considered or misconstrued by others? Maybe something that you may have done that some sanctimonious person or persons might feel inappropriate for the church setting?"

Myra-Ann gave the girls a curt expression as everyone smothered in silence. "Are you serious?" She challenged. "Our sole purpose is to praise the Lord in dance. Unless there's some jealous haters out there, I cannot think of any reason for this obvious absurd attack on our integrity." Deep within and hidden from the expressions on their face, the dancers were quite aware that their popularity was based more on their performances than on the premise of worshiping God.

Timothy felt his phone buzzing in his pocket. "Excuse me ladies, I have a call. He glanced at his screen; the call was from Pos-I-tive Rhema. "Hello Mr. Widbell, what's up?"

Pos-I-tive stammered, "Most conclusively I will inform you of the malevolent message I received."

"Woe, don't tell me you received a message from the Psalmist?"

Hazela blurted, "Oh Lord, did someone else get a message? Who is that?"

Timothy signaled her to be quiet as he said, "Mr. Widbell, would you kindly hold the line for a minute?" He placed the phone on mute and then informed, "This call is from Mr. Widbell."

Myra-Ann was perplexed. "Just who is Mr. Widbell?"

Timothy informed, "Well, you probably know him as Pos-I-tive Rhema."

With panic creeping into her voice, Karoln groaned, "No, don't tell me that he got one too. What's this all about?"

Timothy said, "Hold on ladies, let me finish this call." He un-muted the phone. "Now Mr. Widbell, can you relay exactly what the message said, okay?"

Pos-I-tive Rhema took a deep breath and informed, "This is a direct quote: *'Your words are merely vanity of vanities. Hear me now, 'The beginning of his talk is folly, and the end of his talk is mischievous madness.' Ecclesiastes 10:13 Son of Yahweh's True Psalmist.'* Listen, Mr. Samuels, I feel no ways threatened or compromised by this sardonic individual. I merely wanted to keep you abreast as to what is going on."

"Alright sir, we'll meet up at the Convention in Cincinnati, bye."

"Blessings to you, my assiduous friend." The two terminated the conversation.

Timothy then focused his attention back on the dance group. "Now ladies, let's discuss your situation."

"Oh no," Myra-Ann blurted. "What's exactly going on with Pos-I-tive Rhema. We have a right to know what's going on. We're all in the same boat now."

Hazela echoed, "That's right, don't keep us in the dark."

"Listen, so far from what Mr. Widbell has told me, everything is cool. Nothing has happened to him."

Florance interjected, "You mean, nothing has happened yet."

"That's right," Karoln broke in.

"Come on, ladies. So far things have been, shall I say, safe for most of us." The phone rang again with another call from Pos-I-tive Rhema. He let the phone ring several times.

Myra-Ann flatly called out in a whisper, "Well, ain't you going to answer that, Mr. Samuels?"

Timothy agreed, and then responded to Pos-I-tive Rhema. "Hello, Mr. Widbell, is everything alright? We just talked."

Florance insisted in hushed tones, "Mr. Samuels, if that's Pos-I-tive Rhema, we all want to hear what the real deal is."

"Yeah," Hazela insisted. "Put it on speaker-phone so we all can hear."

He nodded his head in agreement. "What's up, Mr. Widbell?"

Pos-I-tive's voice was wavering which was a clear indication that he was unsettled. "Is it okay if I call you Tim? Since we're going to have to jointly oppose this adversity together, we had better be on a more amicable plane."

When Florance parted her lips to say something, Timothy signaled her to hush. "Okay, you must have more to tell me."

"Perhaps I was feeling a bit too much fortuitous when we spoke a few moments ago."

"Uh-huh," Timothy grunted.

"Well Tim, my wife just informed me that our website, Facebook, Twitter, and You Tube accounts have been hacked. In fact, we are genuinely under a serious cyber-attack. We have been flooded with ominous emails to our personal email accounts. Thank the Almighty that our bank accounts have not been affected so far. Perhaps I was too nonchalant about the entire situation. My wife and I will strive to be resilient regarding this matter, however we must vindicate your efforts to get to the bottom of the Yahweh's True Psalmist situation. Please be advised that we will buttress and undergird you totally in your approach to crush this hedonist demagogue. We will spare no expense to rid us of this culprit. We shall collaborate when we meet in Cincinnati."

Timothy in a reassuring voice, "Sure, together we will get to the bottom of this whole affair." The two concluded the phone call as Timothy glanced as Ceremonious appeared to be doing some self-examination with trepidation and fear clearly painted on their faces.

Hazela raised her hand, as if she were a student in class asking the teacher a question. "Timothy, are you sure that was Pos-I-tive Rhema? I mean, it surely didn't sound like him."

Timothy confided, "Pos-I-tive is Mr. Widbell stage name and his professional persona." The four ladies scanned each other's facial expressions and then simultaneously peered at Timothy. "Ladies," Timothy hinted. "Now is the time for us to figure out why we're being singled out."

With some indignation, Myra-Ann smirked, "We can't think of any reason, right girls? Well, am I right?"

"Perhaps," Hazela indicated. "We might need to pray a little more."

Florance, Karoln, Hazela and even Timothy echoed, "Amen."

Chapter 17

"All Alone In The Wilderness of The True Anointment"

"FOR LOVE IS STRONG AS DEATH;
JEALOUSY IS CRUEL AS THE GRAVE."
SONG OF SOLOMON 8:6A

Karen once again proved to Timothy Samuels that she could forgive him and address the real pressing issues that they faced. He was stunned to see her number on caller ID as he rushed to catch the flight from O'Hare International Airport. "Karen," he beamed. "I'm so glad to hear from you."

Sarcastically she responded, "Are you really?"

"Girl, you know I've been calling constantly since the last time I saw you." He glanced at his watch which indicated that he had to hustle to make his flight to Philadelphia. "Karen, I'm on my way to Philly right now." He began running and she could hear him panting as he dodged the masses of people in the terminal.

"Why are you breathing so hard?" She teasingly asked him. "You must really be excited about talking to me."

"Yes, I'm extremely excited," he admitted. "I'm late for my flight," he puffed. "Listen, is it alright if I come by as soon as I get in town? Oh, and by the way, how are the kids?"

"They're fine, you'd better hurry up and catch that flight. We'll talk when you get here. How did things work out with the hoochie- coochie dancers?"

"Now, come on. It was all business. By the way, Pos-I-tive has informed me that he has received a message from the Psalmist. Look, I've got to hang up and check my bags. I'll catch you later."

"Alright Tim," she chirped. "You'd better come straight here and don't you dare divert to Brooklyn to see Pos-I-tive Rhema. Your children are anxious to see you."

He didn't bother to comment on her use of the word '*your children*'. He had to finally rationalized that he had to consider Johnnie just as much his son as he knew she deemed Teresa her daughter.

He was delighted that she seemed to have forgiven him for his misdeeds. He actually felt that he was blessed to have her for a friend. He quickly checked his bags and somehow managed to make his flight on time.

He had booked a business class seat and was just settling in when he received a text message just prior to the jet taking off. He read the following message from Zachariah Phillips:

123

'Call 911 situation '. He was not able to respond to the text because the flight attendant cautioned him to turn off his phone and all electronic devices.

Timothy was becoming apprehensive regarding the 911 meaning of the text message. His mind was in a whirlpool with worry. He now understood why Karen may have been so agitated when he chose to rush to Ceremonious when his own love ones may have had a greater need. He finally calmed himself when he rationalized that he had just concluded a conversation with Karen no more than a half an hour ago. He eventually relaxed when he realized that there was nothing he could do from thousands of feet in the air. He glanced at the Sky Mall magazine and then succumb to sleep as the jet cruised toward his destination.

As he slumbered during the two hours and forty-five-minute flight, the Psalmist's had made another antagonistic anonymous contact. This time the message was sent to the Smoley Sisters from Lexington, Kentucky. They were usually headlined as The Celestial Smoley Sisters. They were the top female group in the Gospel music industry. The group originally consisted of four sisters with palindromic names that spelled the same frontwards and backwards. The youngest of the sisters, Eve, had journeyed on to be with her Lord a year ago. The three remaining sisters, Hannah, Arora, and Ailia endeavored to keep the group together. Without Eve, their lead singer, the group struggled to connect with each other, and most importantly, with their audience.

Reluctantly, they were forced to recruit their distant cousin, Flora-Bea from Newark, New Jersey into the group. They were well aware that Flora-Bea was a far superior singer than they were. She had a unique voice that was reminiscent of their late sister Eve's voice. The group had recently signed a new recording contract and it was urgent that this group produce a new project immediately.

The three sisters were extremely jealous of Flora-Bea's talent and dynamic stage presence. Their displeasure was camouflaged by their showering her with compliments and covertly insincere praises. Flora-Bea was somewhat naïve, and the false compliments urged her to rally the group to new and greater success. She was altogether unaware of the message that her cousins received from Yahweh's True Psalmist. The Psalmist seemed to be quite aware of their inner feelings toward her. The message that they received in the mail, postmarked from Lexington, Kentucky, threw the group into a tailspin of self-awareness and trepidation. Yahweh's True Psalmist would generally text or e-mail to the targeted artists.

The group immediately contacted Zachariah Phillips, who in turn emailed Timothy a copy of the letter. Timothy and Zachariah were somewhat perplexed due to the fact that the letter had been post marked from the group's hometown address.

Timothy and Zachariah concluded that the Psalmist may have access to the physical addresses and locations of the people he had contacted via emails and text messages. Their reasoning was based on the letter coming from Lexington, and the fact that Amoz's car had been attacked while he dined at a local Red Lobster Restaurant. It appeared to them that the Psalmist had apparently hacked into the data base of the G-POW Convention attendees, star performers, and possibly into Zachariah's personal accounts. It was also evident that the Psalmist was intimately aware of the interpersonal relationships of many of the Gospel artist that he had contacted.

Perhaps the Psalmist was also somehow mindful that whenever Flora-Bea would sing in front of an audience, a glow or an aura seemed to surround her. The other ladies in the group thought that the spotlight was highlighting her more than them. They did not understand that this light was supernatural. It was often referred to as 'God's Shekinah Glory' by the seasoned saints. Shekinah Glory was the presence of God dwelling within her as she ministered in song. The Celestial Smoley Sisters did not understand the significance of reaching people through songs. They had little or no inkling about touching people's lives with an uplifting song and giving God praise simultaneously. Sometimes during a performance, Eve would periodically signal her sisters to stop singing and for the musicians to stop playing music to fraught or hinder what they considered her performance. Unbeknownst to them, Flora-Bea was not performing-she was a true worshipper of God. Consequently, Flora-Bea was able to sing without any assistance from the group, or the musicians. She assumed that the musicians and her cousins' actions were part of their act. To the singing sisters astonished dismay, this form of trickery only ushered in a special anointing upon their cousin and drew more people into a deeper spiritual experience. This consequently caused their popularity to explode. The group was delighted about their ever-increasing success; however, the palindrome sisters' jealousy was increasing exponentially and overshadowing their contempt for Flora-Bea.

The message they received from the Psalmist was clear and blunt with an ominous introduction: *"Saul was jealous of my father's gift from God. I, the Son of Yahweh's True Psalmist am aware of your bitter jealousy. The fate of Saul awaits you. 'For jealousy is the rage of a man; therefore, he will not spare in the day of judgment. Proverbs 6:34'"*

This was the reason the Celestial Smoley Sisters immediately contacted Jeremiah Phillips. He also had been contacted by every major performer of the upcoming convention regarding sinister and menacing threats from either Yahweh's True Psalmist or Son of Yahweh's True Psalmist.

Zachariah Phillips, the Emperor of Gospel Music had just received the following message mailed directly to his local post office box.

> *"There is no one above God. **Jesus is the King of Kings**. A king rules a nation. An emperor rules the kings of nations. An emperor is a king of kings. But the true King of Kings will judge you and His wrath will come upon you. You are a fraud. There is no Emperor of Gospel Music. There are only True Worshippers and you are not one of them. You are a vain fool; you are a present-day wicket King Ahab, and your ministry is Queen Jezebel. 'The kings of the earth set themselves, and the rulers take counsel together against the LORD, and against His anointed... Yahweh's True Psalmist Psalm 2:2'"*

For the first time in his life, Zachariah Phillips, the Emperor of Gospel Music, felt overwhelmed with fear. Despite his numerous testimonies and sermons about his great faith in God, and his vast recordings that encouraged so many to trust in the Lord, he was altogether in an unimaginable panic-bred state of mind.

When Timothy arrived at the apartment, he had to consider his own problems as he dismissed all the dramatic inferences that Zachariah had presented to him. He made arrangements to obtain a rental car and swiftly guided the car to Karen's apartment. To his surprise, Karen darted out the door, wrapped her arms firmly around him causing him to lose grip on his luggage and camera bags. She kissed him more passionately than he had ever experience from her before. Her sudden display of affection startled him somewhat as he tried to free himself from her ever tightening grip.

"Baby," Karen huffed. "What's up with you? You're acting as though you haven't missed me."

Gathering his breath as well as his wits, Timothy gasped, "Now girl, you know I missed you. But baby, ain't this kind of sudden – and a little too public?" He couldn't find the rationale for the sudden and vivid shift in her attitude towards him. *'After all,'* he reasoned. *'The last time I saw her, she practically threw me out of the house.'* He somehow managed to say, "Karen, you know that I missed you, but you seemed to have made a one-hundred-eighty-degree change. Now, don't get me wrong. I like this new attitude, but can we first get into the house so I can check on the kids and tell you what's going on?"

Karen eventually loosened her grip and assisted him as they gathered his belongings. She displayed a non-threatening smirk as the two children bounded into the room with ever so bright smiles painted upon their faces. To Timothy's astonishment, before he and his daughter had a chance to greet each other, Johnnie blurted out, "Daddy!" Timothy was utterly amazed that this child was becoming more verbal. Perhaps his daughter had a greater influence on the little boy than Timothy could ever have envisioned. Timothy realized that the boy was a musical prodigy with speech difficulties, but now he was actually communicating directly with him. He became more bewildered when the boy stuttered and voiced, "I-I-I love, love you, Da-da."

Teresa beamed as she proudly announced, "I've been working with him, Dad. He's really catching on." Timothy felt that perhaps the child was merely echoing words and expressions that he heard from Teresa.

Timothy was practically speechless, but managed to say, "I'm so proud of both of you." In actuality, he was truly touched and amazed. "Well, I'm really impressed with both of you."

As they entered into the kitchen area, Karen offered, "Hey, are you guys ready to eat? I've fixed your favorite, Tim." Timothy nodded as the children rushed to find a place at the table.

"Eat. Eat. Eat." Johnnie repeatedly bellowed to everyone's laughter, as they eyed and sniffed at the food in the center of the table.

"Daddy," Teresa asked as she dipped a spoon into the bowl of potato salad, "How was the trip? Did you really meet Ceremonious? Do they have any new dances? Have you heard any more from the Psalmist?"

Timothy swiftly began to devour a chicken wing as he cautioned her, "Girl, you're firing questions like a county prosecutor." He finished the piece of the chicken, and helped himself to a drumstick, and answered, "Yes, I met the ladies; but they refused to show me any of their praise dances at all."

Karen interjected, "I wouldn't consider them ladies. And I certainly wouldn't call what they do *Praise Dancing*. I'd say it's more like club dancing." Timothy wouldn't let them know that he characterized their dances more like '*Pole Dancing*'

Timothy rolled his eyes as Teresa interjected, "Oh, you two are so old fashion. Right Daddy? And Daddy, when are we leaving for Cincinnati? Me and Johnnie are so excited. He can hardly wait to get on that stage and wail on that Hammond organ."

"Yeah Tim," Karen agreed. "When are we leaving? It's going to take time for me to pack for me and the kids. I have to decide for someone to keep an eye on the apartment, get the mail, and so many other things that mothers have to take care of. The convention is the day after tomorrow. So. when are we leaving?" Timothy managed to display a nondescript expression on his face as he sprinkled Tabasco sauce on his collard greens. Karen waited for a response and then continued, "Well, what have you got to say? Cat got your tongue?"

Timothy had absent mindedly used too much hot sauce and pretended that he was choking as he coughed continually to obviously avoid answering the inquiry. Karen curled her lip, frowned, and taunted, "I guess this is a discussion for you and I after the children go to bed."

Teresa slammed her fork on the table. "Oh no, I'm old enough to get in this conversation too. I'm a teenager, now. You're not leaving me again this time!"

Little Johnnie slammed his fork on the table and blurted, "Me too!"

The LORD's Song In A Strange Land

Chapter 18

"Whose Time? Whose Purpose?"

"TO EVERYTHING THERE IS A SEASON,
AND A TIME TO EVERY PURPOSE UNDER THE HEAVEN."
ECCLESIASTES 3:1

Timothy struggled to change the subject. "You know Karen, I was thinking maybe the G-POW convention is not the right time or place for the children to attend. In fact, it might be safer for you to stay here, and keep the children safe. Baby, I know you really--"

Before he could complete his sentence, Karen cut in, "And watch the children? I guess, I'm just a babysitter now. Oh, so you want more alone time with the dancers and Lord knows who else you may or may not encounter." Karen continued with a smirk. "Is that why you want me and the children to stay here while you go galivanting around Cincinnati? Oh no brother, I'm beginning to wonder if there is a hidden purpose for all your traveling. How do you know whether or not this Psalmist, or Son of Psalmist, or whoever he or she is, might provoke or threaten us while you're hundreds of miles away?"

"No, it's not like that," Timothy protested. "I'm really concerned about the potential safety and well-being issues with the children and you; and not to mention, the potential madness that may occur at the convention. This menacing dude will probably do his mischief at the convention. He can't be in two places at once, now can he? You all will be safer here."

Karen suggested, "Suppose that there is more than one person playing this Yahweh's True Psalmist or Son of Yahweh's True Psalmist. Haven't the messages that he sent tagged with two different names? Maybe several people consist of Yahweh's True Psalmist and Son of Yahweh's True Psalmist. This could even be a team or group of people. We just don't know. I feel that Zachariah Phillips should involve the law enforcement. You are not the police, or even a detective. So, you see, we should all go together as a team and look out for each other. Well, I guess that settles it, doesn't it?"

Timothy pondered for a while, and then protested, "I don't think this so-called Emperor of Gospel Music wants any law enforcement intervention. In spite of the dangers implied, sometimes he seems to delight in the fact that my blogs and photos have increased interest in the convention. Not only that, but tickets sales have also gone through the roof and ticket scalpers are making like bandits. I am also making surprisingly good money for us all."

134

Almost simultaneously Karen and Teresa pushed their plates aside, stood up, and rumbled loudly, "We're going." Karen emphasized, "I'm not kidding. I mean it, and that's final."

Johnnie echoed, "We going! Final! Final! We going!" He began flapping his hands indicating that the apparent tension was responsible for his stimming behavior. Johnnie's uncontrollable shedding of tears also began to draw their focus to him. He continued flapping both of his arms more violently. This resulted in a gradual cease to their outspoken disagreement.

Karen and Teresa were well acquainted to handle Johnnie during these particular episodes. Karen comforted him by gently holding his left hand while stroking his head gently. Teresa slowly approached him and eased both hands around his right hand, looked him directly into his eyes, and whispered, "Would you play a song for me and I'll sing. Okay, Johnnie? You play so nicely."

"No," he snapped. "Want to go. Want to go. We going. Final"

Teresa lowered her whispering to a practically almost soundless urging, "Please Johnnie, I need you to play to help me sing."

"Yes," Karen added. "Go play for Teresa."

Timothy taking the hint, "Yes Johnnie, go play for Teresa."
Apparently, Johnnie did not like the sound and timbre of
Timothy's voice and commenced returning to flapping his
hands and making various groans and utterances.

Karen and Teresa gave Timothy a stern look of disapproval.
"Hush, Daddy. We can handle him. You're not around
enough to understand him. " Karen continued cautiously
rubbing his head in circular motions until he eventually
became practically motionless and tranquil. Karen loosened
her slight grip on his hand, motioned for him to follow
Teresa, and then breathed a sigh of relief as the children
exited the kitchen.

Timothy and Karen could hear Teresa singing *'Yes, Jesus
Loves Me'* as Johnnie skillfully followed every note in great
precision. The two adults remained hushed for a few
moments until Karen took the initiative, opened a drawer in
the kitchen, handed Timothy a notebook and a pen, and
indicated, "Why don't you make a chart about all of these
people, not including us, that have received some type of
contact, indirect or direct from this character. Okay? Then
we can intelligently assess the situation."

Timothy reflected on her suggestion, "That's a great idea.
I'll need your help, of course. In fact, I will try to tie the
direct threats with the communications and the photos that
I've taken. Wow, that's a tremendous idea." He began to
refer to his notes written haphazardly on sheets of paper

scattered in his camera bags and luggage. I really don't know where to begin. Perhaps I should start with my uncle, Bishop Graystien because he alerted me to get me the assignment. But I don't think he received any contact from the Psalmist."

Karen gave him a reassuring glance. "Tim, I think we can skip assessing the bishop. After all, didn't Zachariah contact the bishop, and then the bishop suggested to him that he use your services? I think that would imply that Bishop Graystien should be in the clear. I think we need to concentrate on the artists that may have been threatened, and also attempt to figure out if there are any connections to us."

"Sounds good to me", Timothy confirmed. "I don't hear the children making music."

"Maybe they went to sleep."

"I doubt it," Timothy advised as Teresa entered the room excitedly.

"So, Dad, are we still going?" She trilled. "Are we?"

Johnnie entered carrying his Yamaha Portable keyboard smiling broadly and chorused, "Going. We Going?"

Karen reassured them, "We're working on it. Now Johnnie you go to bed in your room and get some sleep. Teresa you can go to the guest room too."

137

"Okay, Karen. But that's not a guest room. It's my room. Oh, and Daddy, I'm going to need some new clothes."

Timothy smirked, nodded, and conceded, "We'll see. We're working on it, and we will just see which way the cat throws her tail?"

Teresa let out a laugh and somehow manage to say, "What does cats have to do with this?"

Karen instructed, "That's something old people say. Now, you go on to bed and let us grown-folks figure out which way this cat will throw its tail."

"Well, I guess," Timothy hinted. "I'd better change my hotel reservation to make room for all of us."

"Dad, I like the way this cat throws its tail" Teresa beamed and slowly made her way to her room.

Karen gave them both an approving glance, "Yeah, I think the cat's throwing the tail in the right direction."

Chapter 19

"Writing Progressions"

"WRITE THEM UPON THE TABLE OF THINE HEART"
PROVERBS 7:3B

Karen handed Timothy a cup of light and sweet coffee. She knew how he liked his coffee. She often teased him that he actually liked a little coffee to flavor his cream and sugar. As he concluded his seventh call, she thought it would be a good time to check on his progress. "Baby," she purred. "Did you find us a place? I guess most, if not all the hotels were pretty much booked."

"Yeah," he conveyed. "There's a possibility we can get a suite at the Cincinnati Convention Center. There might be something available due to a cancellation. Then when the convention is over, we can probably take the kids to the aquarium. It's not too far from the hotel. Right now, I'm just waiting for the hotel to call me back to confirm the reservation."

"That's great. I guess we can start packing tomorrow."

"Yeah, but I'm going to have to get a larger car, so would you contact Enterprise and upgrade us to a larger vehicle, maybe a mini-van or a SUV."

"Okay, I'm on it". As she dialed the car rental company, she heard his phone signal that a call was coming. "Maybe it's about our suite."

"No, it's Zachariah. "I'd better pick it up."

"Just let it ring. We might lose our hotel reservation."

He ignored her request, "Hello, Mr. Phillips. How can I help you?"

Karen peered at him as she signaled with her hands for him to hang up, and then gingerly urged, "Hang up, he probably has more crazy assignments for you to rush off to."

"Hush. Oh no, not you Mr. Phillips. Could I call you back, I have a call on the other line?" Karen's ear seemed to perk up when she heard about the incoming call. She signaled again for him to hang up.

Zachariah Phillips continued, "No Timothy, this is important. Whoever or whatever is on the other line, can wait. You know the convention is the day after tomorrow. I think I may have found a solution for our predicament." Timothy was a little astonished and listened intensively. "I'm not saying that I'm one hundred percent sure," Zachariah insisted, "but I do have a solid suspicion."

Timothy allowed his call on hold to go to voice mail. "Wow," Timothy assured. "I'm really impressed with your detective skills. I suppose you won't need me to do much more research."

"No Brother Tim," Zachariah insisted, "I didn't say that this situation is over. I merely have a theory. Let me explain, Okay?"

"Sure," Timothy indicated with mild enthusiasm.

Karen tapped Timothy on his shoulder and softly urged, "What's going on? You look a little excited."

Timothy muted the phone and acknowledged, "He thinks he may know who the Psalmist is." He unmuted and then focused his entire attention on Zachariah Phillips.

Zachariah continued. "Timothy, I don't want you to devolve the details to anyone, understand?"

"Yeah sure," Timothy confirmed.

Zachariah continued. "You see, everyone that's scheduled to perform at the conclusion of the convention has received some form of contact, message, and even threats from this adversary. Everyone except for one group."

Timothy began to review the performers that he was
associated with since he first met Zachariah. As Zachariah
recalled the performers, he took notes with the paper that
Karen had handed him:

> **Zachariah Phillips** – *The Emperor of Gospel
> Music-Impresario and Founder of the Gospel Performers
> of The World (G-POW)*
>
> *His son,* **Amoz Phillips** *Multi-Talented Soloist*
>
> **Joktan Jahnson, Jr.**, *the so-called Archduke Soloist*
>
> **Pos-i-tive Rehema** – *Gospel Rapper*
>
> **Ceremonious** *-Liturgical Dance Troupe*
>
> **The Celestial Smoley Sisters**-*Female Vocal Group*

Timothy confirmed, "I took notes of everyone you mentioned. Do
you think that someone on this list is a suspect?"

"Actually Tim, " Zachariah confessed. "I haven't been straight
forward with you. There is one act that I never mentioned to you.
I didn't mention them to you because they never received any
contact at all from Yahweh's True Psalmist or Son of Yahweh's
True Psalmist. Timothy did you notice that something was
missing from the notes you just took?"

"Well, not really. I wrote down everything you said."

"Then I guess I will have to make you think about it. Read over
your list to yourself, and then ask yourself what type of Gospel
performer is not on your list."

Timothy took a guess. "I don't see gospel mimes on your list. To
be perfectly honest with you, I hate Gospel mimes, and I'm glad

they weren't on the list. So maybe, the missing link is gospel mimes."

Zachariah let out a chuckle, "I couldn't allow mimes on the same stage with Ceremonious. Those ladies are extremely envious of other non-verbal performers. Besides that, I don't care for mimes either. I have arranged for some mimes to perform, but not on the culmination of the convention. I won't keep you in suspense to much longer. Let me clarify this first. I was beginning to be tempted to call the authorities, like the police, or the FBI. But perhaps, I thought if we put our heads together, we could solve this mystery ourselves without outside intervention. After all, the local police will handle the security in the Conference Center. I wanted you to use all of your skills and information to verify this culprit and expose him to the entire G-POW organization. Any negative press from this could ruin the entire convention. Too many people have worked too hard to make this a success."

Timothy felt that Zachariah was probably more concerned about losing money, and he also knew that people were already aware of some of the antics of Yahweh's True Psalmist. It was too difficult to keep all this drama from spreading by word of mouth and hints from Timothy's blog. He muted his phone again and motioned for Karen to come near him. "Baby contact the hotel. Scroll through my contact book and get the number. The reservation is under my name."

After unmuting his phone, "Sir, if you think you know who's responsible, then what can I do? Perhaps, more importantly, what can we do? And you've still haven't told me much. Perhaps there is a genre that's missing."

Zachariah was relishing in the fact that Timothy hadn't been able to figure out the simplest answer. " You're getting warm, now. Suppose this was an old-school R and B show. Who would you like to see perform?"

Timothy was slightly upset that he was being quizzed and toyed with, but he managed to play along. "I'd say, *The Temptations, The Four Tops, Mary Wells, The Supremes, Martha and The Vandellas ,Al Green, The Moments, The Stylistics, The Dells, The O'Jay's,* and so many others. I could go on and on. "

"Well Brother," Zachariah encouraged. "You're getting even warmer."

A sense of accomplishment showered over Timothy's face. "I think I got it. I think I figured it out."

"Well then tell me," Zachariah urged.

"I did not hear you mention a male group. You know, a Gospel quartet. That makes a lot of sense. A group of men. A quartet! Am I right? If I'm right, tell me. Do I know this group? Are they real popular?"

144

Zachariah Phillips, The Emperor of Gospel music admitted, "Yes sir, you hit the nail right on the top of the head. I don't think anyone really knows a lot about these guys. They are an up and coming group that I put on the program at the last minute and gave them top billing with the other artists. They were heavily funded by a sponsor. If you don't mind, I will quote you one of my favorite Scriptures. *'A feast is for laughter, and wine maketh merry: but money answereth all things. Ecclesiastes 10:9'* And before you think about it, I am NOT the Psalmist just because I quoted the writings from one of the books that the so-called Yahweh's True Psalmist uses. The group's name is *Chosen Cherub.* To be honest with you, they practically sponsored the entire event by paying for the venue and providing me with a large honorarium."

It didn't take Timothy long to conclude that this Emperor of Gospel Music is all about the money and nothing else. Timothy thought, *'If he felt that The Chosen Cherub was responsible for all this confusion and trouble, why didn't he just expose them.'* Timothy remember a Bible Scripture or was it a song by the O'Jays that included the words: *'For the love of money'.*

 Zachariah concluded, "Please check this out as soon as you get to Cincinnati. They've rented a large house just outside of the city. I'll forward their address and contact information in my next text. They seemed to be loaded with money. I have to admit that they are the largest financial sponsors of the entire G-POW Convention."

"Solid, Mr. Phillips. I will also research their style of music, genre, and so forth."

"Before we hang up," Zachariah added. "Do some research on the musical progressions that I will text you. I heard you really like old style doo-wop music; I will send you the basic chord progression for that type of music and a few other progressions including traditional blues, and Gospel music. Then finally, I will send you the chord progression that Chosen Cherub uses. Note, all their songs begin in the key of D Sharp, progress to D Natural, and conclude in D Flat. Also, Google *Chosen Cherub*. When you've done with that research, then you may conclude why I've become wary of this group and feel they may be responsible for this Yahweh's True Psalmist nonsense. Bless you man, see you in Cincinnati."

When the call concluded, Karen was extremely inquisitive about what had transpired. He decided to share her questions for a later time as she informed him, "We've got the reservation all set. We'll have a deluxe two-bedroom suite, and you'll be sleeping on the couch. Get use to the couch because that's where you're bunking tonight. Uhh, by the way, do you feel like telling me what's going on?"

Timothy smirked and said, "Not now. You've got a lot to do, why don't you call it a day and I'll fill you in tomorrow."

"Tim, aren't you going to rest now? You had that long flight and you're probably beat."

"No, I've got a lot of research to do. A whole lot of research."

"I'll see you in the morning," she managed to say as she exited the room. She was somewhat disappointed that Timothy would need more coaxing for the questions she would like to have answered.

"Yeah Karen," he managed to say as he began to Google *Chosen Cherub* on his phone. His search led him to Ezekiel 28:14-16. *'Man,'* he thought. *'I only know that Ezekiel saw some type of wheel in the sky. I'm not digging into this Old Testament Bible stuff. Sometimes this stuff creeps me out. I'll just call my uncle Bishop Graystien in the morning.'*

He then opened the text that he received from Zachariah Phillips and became more confused when he read:

Common Chord Progressions:

I-V-vi-IV

I-vi-IV-V

I-I-I-I-IV-IV-I-I-V-I-I

Chosen Cherub Chord Progression in

The Keys of D sharp, modulating to D natural,

Finally modulating to D flat:

I-II-V-I (Rest -Repeat)

147

Timothy powered his phone off and mumbled, *'I thought Ezekiel's spinning intertwined wheels in the sky had me confused, but this is even more ridiculous.'*

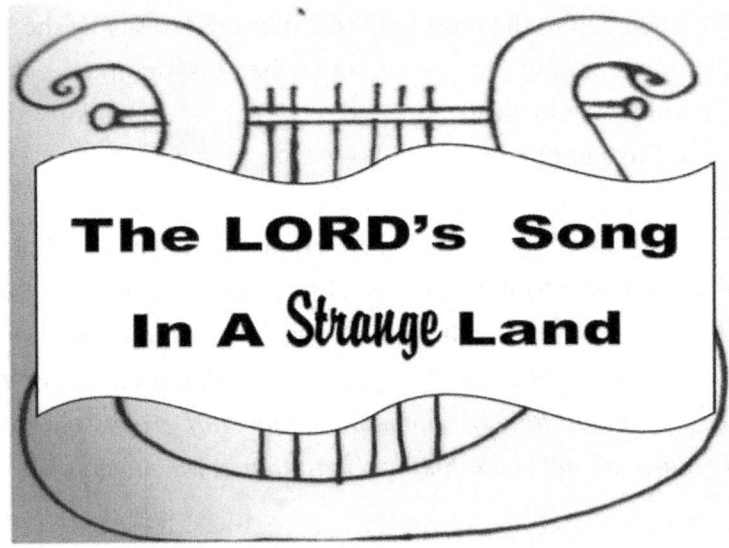

Chapter 20

"Not Understanding The Answers"

"A SERVANT WILL NOT BE CORRECTED BY WORDS:
FOR THOUGH HE UNDERSTAND HE WILL NOT ANSWER."
PROVERBS 29:19

Karen took the children shopping for incidentals for the trip. Timothy planned to leave for Cincinnati in a few hours and instructed her to be home by 11:00 A.M. with an expected arrival at the hotel between 9:00 and 9:30 P.M. Timothy had packed his equipment, most of the luggage and he needed some private time to decipher the information that he received from Zachariah Phillips.

He planned to contact his uncle, Bishop Graystien to obtain some information about the Biblical aspects of the meaning and significance of Chosen Cherub. He wondered why a quartet would have acquired a singular noun for a plural group. He was aware of the use of collective nouns for words such as *team, crew,* and *people,* but he pondered, *'Why aren't they known as the Chosen Cherubs, plural, instead of Cherub, singular? Why was Zachariah so mysterious about the whole Chosen Cherub thing? I still have my cautious distrust of this so-called Emperor of Gospel Music. I'm still under the impression that he may be using this whole scenario as a means of gaining more publicity. However, if he wants me to keep this new information on the down-low, for all I know, the real culprits might actually be this newly discovered mysterious Gospel quartet.'*

Karen's personal ringtone on his phone interrupted his chain of thoughts. "Yes Karen, what's up? How's the shopping going? You know we have to get on the road soon."

Karen curtly responded, "I know. I know. We should be home soon. I will pick up some snacks to eat on the way at Giant Supermarket. Is there anything special that you would like? I should be back in about an hour or so. Would you like to say something to the kids?"

"Sure, tell them I said 'hello'. Don't worry about me, I'll munch on whatever you bring back. Oh yeah, tell them I miss them and I'm excited about the trip."

Teresa cut in, "We can hear you, Dad. We miss you too."

Johnnie added, "Miss you Dad. Pretzels from Giant."

"Okay Karen, I've got a lot of research and calls to make, so let's talk later, bye."

Karen and the children let out a chorus of "Good-byes," which ended the conversation.

It was now time for him to focus on gaining more data about Chosen Cherub. He felt that if anyone could give him some insight on the Chosen Cherub, it would be his friend, Lee-Ray Harris. Lee-Ray was a bonified expert on all types of music, particularly in the Gospel music field. Though Timothy knew that if anyone could enlighten him, Lee-Ray could; however, he required financial compensation for the inanest or even more profound information he would impart. He made the decision to just pay whatever fee he requested. *'After all,'* he thought. *'I'm not paying for this. It will come out of my expense account.'* "Hey Lee, I need your help. Have you got a few moments to spare?"

"Well Timmy, what's up?" Lee-Ray responded in his usual nonchalant manner. "Are you still working on that G-POW matter? So, what can I do for you?"

Timothy was slightly shocked that Lee-Ray didn't immediately mention finances, but he knew money was somewhere planted in the back of Lee-Ray Harris' mind. "Yeah, I'm still on the case. Listen, can you fill me in a little on a Gospel quartet known as Chosen Cherub?"

The nonchalant tone of his voice was gradually shipping into business mode. "How much information do you need? You know my time is expensive."

Timothy hid his displeasure of Lee-Roy's apparent acquisitive manner. "Look, Lee-Ray, you name the price. I haven't got much time. I'm leaving for Cincinnati in about an hour."

"Okay," Lee-Ray said. "How about $150, and I'll give you a brief world tour of information. Is that alright?"

Timothy agreed, "That's fine. Also, for that amount, I want you to tell me a little about chord progressions."

Lee-Ray groaned, "Now that will be another $50. Okay?"

Timothy was becoming increasingly agitated, but he consented. "Man, I told you I don't have much time, just lay it on me."

A look of contentment eased out of Lee-Ray's voice, "Now, there's not a lot to be said about Chosen Cherub. They're a relatively new group in the modern Gospel scene. These guys are totally different from any group I've ever heard. I'm talking about Gospel, jazz, R and B. You name it, these guys use it all and are off the chain. I can't characterize their sound or place it in any group that I've heard before. They somehow seem to have a cult like following. I don't dig their sounds, man, it's too repetitious."

Timothy interjected, "Well, a lot of this new Gospel music is very repetitious. Sometimes they say the same thing over and over."

Though Timothy couldn't observe it, Lee-Ray nodded his head in agreement. "Man, this is totally repetitious on a whole new level, a whole new stratosphere, and a whole new planet. In fact, they're on a whole new universe. Their sound is quite nauseating in my esteemed opinion."

Timothy was becoming intensely intrigue by the possibility of this group having a cult-like following. "Tell me what makes them so unique? Why would you claim they have a cult-like following? Does it have anything to do with their chord progressions?"

"Yeah, that has a lot to do with it," Lee-Ray agreed. "Most, if not many songs, follow some type of chord progressions."

Timothy had earlier texted him a copy of the chord progressions that Zachariah had sent him. "Explain the chord progressions that I just sent you. Tell me how they relate to Chosen Cherub."

Lee-Ray continued, "Actually, it's not just the chord progression, it's the fact that every single song uses the exact same progression. It reminds me of some of the doo-wop progression used constantly in the 1950's and early 60's. You know songs like *Duke of Earl, Stand by Me, and Please Mister Poster* used a common progression. There are literally hundreds or perhaps thousands of songs that use the One-Six Minor-Four-Five progression. Including many Gospel songs."

"Okay" Timothy cut-in", but what makes their progression so unique?"

Lee-Ray continued, "It's their constant repetitiveness and modulating down as opposed to modulating up in chromatic half steps. In a lot of Gospel songs, excitement is built on in a song by raising the key in small, or chromatic steps. Chosen Cherub's songs don't build up in half steps, they go down in half-steps. This lowers the tone which puts a more sinister or hypnotic effect on the listeners and especially their cult followers. Their vocal arrangements and use of odd instrumentation are enhanced by their use of Korg Kronos Music Workstation keyboards. These are some really high-tech instruments. They use Kronos almost exclusively – and Kronos is the god of time. The four guys are geniuses who work as though there are totally in sync with one another."

Timothy inserted, "What's so special about that?"

"Dude stop interrupting me, and I'll explain. Most Gospel quartets use guitars, keyboards, and drums. Not these guys, they all stand in a straight line using their Korg Kronos Music Station keyboards to emulate myriad sounds, that for some strange reason puts their fans in a narcotic or shall I say, hypnotic type trance."

"Woe, that sounds spooky."

"Now, check this out. All of their songs have a pause between the progressions. During this pause, the guys exchange positions on the instruments. It's like musical chairs, but with everyone finding an instrument to keep the song going without missing a single beat. Listen man, I've got one more thing to point out. It's the notes that they use that freaks me out. All their songs are in some variant of the key of D. When you write the notes out and include the pauses, the notes always spell a word. It's not like having A-C-E as your chord progression and spell the word 'ACE'. Or B-E-D spelling 'BED'. Every single one of their chord progressions spell 'DEAD' over and over. It's like they're giving a subliminal message to those of us that have a keen ear or perfect pitch. One last thing: after each performance, the group leaves one of the Korg keyboards on stage as what they characterize as their 'Sacrifice' to Yah." He abruptly terminated the conversation. "That's it, your time is up, Bro, you know how to send my fee through Zelle. I'll check my bank for the fee. Catch you later, I've got another call on the line."

Timothy just stared at the phone as he tried to digest this information, he reasoned, *'I guess Bishop Graystien will complete the picture with the spiritual aspects of all this group's odd behavior. He'll have to expound on verses from Ezekiel.'*

After Timothy devoured the last bit of lunch meat and crusty whole wheat bread, he dialed his uncle, Bishop Graystien. He was delighted to hear his booming baritone voice burst

155

through his earpiece. "Blessings on you my illustrious nephew. How's the G-POW assignment going?"

To appease his uncle's religiosity, he responded, "Well Uncle Bishop Graystien, I'm blessed. Everything is going great except for one little detail that I need your input on."

"Alright," Bishop Graystien assured. "I'm ready to help you. I must assume, knowing you, that it's has something to do with the Bible. My 'Spiritual Antenna' will probably confirm it's no doubt about Chosen Cherub. Zachariah Phillips may have given me a heads-up. Now, what can I do for you?"

Timothy had to admit, "You're right on as usual, Bishop. I just need to know why I was pointed to Ezekiel 28?"

"Tim, I'll just try to give you my simplified exegesis explanation. Cherub is a type of angel. In Ezekiel 10, they are described as having four faces. That may explain why Chosen Cherub consists of four members. Their father was tragically killed under mysterious circumstances. His demise however, left them quite wealthy with a large endowment. What is also interesting about these four brothers, is that they were born fraternal or perhaps identical quadruplets. That may explain the 'four faces' of the Cherub in Ezekiel 10."

"Go head Bishop, you really have my attention."

"Now, let me make the Chosen Cherub connection to these young men. A cherub is a kind of angel. Many theologians consider angels, including cherub, pluralized as cherubim to be considered good or evil angels. Not all angels can be classified as good. According to Revelation chapter 12, verses 7 through 12, a war broke out in Heaven. Ezekiel 28, Isaiah 14, Jude 6, and Second Peter verse 2, verse 4 make reference to this. One-third of the angels were excluded from Heaven with Satan as the ruler of these falling angels. We consider these fallen angels to be demons . Some theologians consider the Chosen Cherub to be Satan, who was excluded from Heaven. Now, let me just read these verses from Ezekiel 28:12-17:

12 Son of man, take up a lamentation upon the king of Tyrus, and say unto him, Thus saith the Lord GOD; Thou sealest up the sum, full of wisdom, and perfect in beauty.

13 Thou hast been in Eden the garden of God; every precious stone was thy covering, the sardius, topaz, and the diamond, the beryl, the onyx, and the jasper, the sapphire, the emerald, and the carbuncle, and gold: the workmanship of thy tabrets and of thy pipes was prepared in thee in the day that thou wast created.

14 Thou art the anointed cherub that covereth; and I have set thee so: thou wast upon the holy mountain of God; thou hast walked up and down in the midst of the stones of fire.

15 Thou wast perfect in thy ways from the day that thou wast created, till iniquity was found in thee.

16 By the multitude of thy merchandise they have filled the midst of thee with violence, and thou hast sinned: therefore I will cast thee as profane out of the mountain of God: and I will destroy thee, O covering cherub, from the midst of the stones of fire.

17 Thine heart was lifted up because of thy beauty, thou hast corrupted thy wisdom by reason of thy brightness: I will cast thee to the ground, I will lay thee before kings, that they may behold thee.

157

You can no doubt tell that the chosen cherub was probably a negative personality, based upon a good interpretation of the quoted Scriptures, but you may make your own decision based on your research and interpretation. You have to decide whether Chosen Cherub quartet is of God or of Satan. To be frank with you and to all intents and purposes, I can't be judgmental in this matter, or for the matter of Yahweh's True Psalmist. Who can reasonably state who is of God or the devil without a direct discernment as concrete proof? So far, I haven't received a discernment in this matter."

Timothy was more confused than ever before. *'I think my uncle was just wrapping an enigma in a tightly rounded conundrum to make me study the Scriptures more.'*

Chapter 21

"Sin Is Nasty"

"THEY RETURN AT EVENING: THEY MAKE NOISE LIKE A DOG
AND GO AROUND ABOUT THE CITY."
Psalm 59:6

Karen merged the Toyota Sienna min-van down the interstate highway west toward Cincinnati as Timothy and the children slept soundly. She estimated that they should arrive at the hotel in about three to four hours. Timothy had done most of the driving up to this point, and was exhausted, not just from the trip, but from the stress of the G-POW Convention starting on tomorrow.

Every attendee of the convention was staying at the Cincinnati Convention Center or local hotels in the greater Cincinnati area. Chosen Cherub, on the other hand, decided to rent a mansion in nearby Florence, Kentucky. The four brothers were all named after archangels: Michael, Raphael, Gabriel, and Jophiel. The brothers were fraternal but bore such a strong resemblance that most people thought they were identical. They relished in fooling and confusing people by dressing alike and having similar behaviors and characteristics. They all participated equally in the creative process however, Michael apparently assumed the leadership role of the group by virtue of him being the first born.

Michael was arranging their premier selection for their finale performance. There were some disagreements and debates regarding the harmony arrangements, exchanging keyboard movements, and also the lyrics to the song. Jophiel was the most adamant about changing the lyrics, but he was overruled by his brothers.

Jophiel protested, "I think these lyrics are taking it too far, guys. We may begin to lose our core fans and probably upset everyone else. I mean we always tried to have subliminal messages, but this is too much."

Raphael disagreed, "Look, we're trying to make a mark in this industry. We are all part of an industry as well as a ministry. We are out to make as much money as we can, and yet inspire people to question the traditional church values." Raphael cut into their discussion, "Guys, I just received a call from the agent that leased us this house. As part of their concierge service, they're catering a mini banquet for us. The food should arrive in about an hour. They also ordered a fruit basket to snack on after we've demolished the food."

Michael grinned and noted, "That's great I was just about to call and have *Door Dash* deliver some bar-b-que."

"Sounds good to me," Jophiel said. "We can deal with the lyrics after we get something in our stomachs. Are you guys ready to eat?"

The other three brothers echoed, "Yeah."

An hour later Raphael utilized the security system's camera and observed a delivery man carrying a huge custom decorated fruit basket. He met the young man at the door, let him in, and escorted him into the kitchen. The young man thanked him as he handed him two twenty-dollar bills. "Sir," Raphael asked, "Do you know when the other food is arriving?"

The Young Man replied, "No sir, a third party phoned this order in and gave us delivery instructions."

Gabriel removed the cellophane from the basket, sampled some grapes and said, "Thanks man. These grapes are really good."

The Young Man nodded, "You're welcome, I've got other deliveries. This is a real nice place. I wish I could stay longer." As the Young Man was escorted out the door an Elderly Man struggled to balance several boxes of food at the top of the stairs. The young man offered, "Do you need any help?"

The Old Man smiled, "Thank you so much. There're two more boxes in my van. Would you mind helping me bring them upstairs?"

The Young Man without hesitation bounded up and down the stairs returning with a box on each trip. The Old Man thanked him again as he watched the Young Man drive off in his car.

The Old Man inquired, "Where do you want me to put the food? Where's the dining area?"

The four brothers waved him away as they gathered the boxes and bought them into the dining area. Michael showed his appreciation to the Old Man by handing him one crisp fifty- dollar bill. "Thank you so much, young man. I hope you enjoy your food."

"Oh, we will," Jophiel assured as he led him out of the house and watched him slowly descend the steps and get into a white cargo van.

The Old Man parked the van in a secluded area of the parking lot of a nearby *Cracker Barrel.* He checked his surroundings, removed the large sunglasses which camouflaged the majority of his upper face. He then removed a fedora hat with a large brim. He chuckled as he removed his oversized gray wig. He applied some baby wipes to remove the makeup that made him appear years older than his actual age. He let out a howling laugh as he removed a bottle of MiraLax from the glovebox. *'I hope the Chosen Cherub enjoys their feast,'* he chuckled. *'I hope they also have lots of toilet paper. This MiraLax should make some interesting music in those six and half bathrooms. I wonder if they will swap places like they do in their concerts. The wonders of science, creating an odorless, tasteless laxative just for my purpose. Enjoy your feast, Chosen Cherubs. Compliments of Yahweh's True Psalmist'.* Two hours later he gleefully sent Michael this text: *'Are you*

*really Yahweh's Chosen Cherub? Who chose you? I hope
you enjoyed your food. 'A poor man that oppresseth the poor
is like sweeping rain which leaveth no food.' Proverbs 28:3.
Son of Yahweh's True Psalmist.'*

All the performances for the final performance of the
G-POW Convention were sold out with standing room only
available. Timothy, Karen, and the kids were settled in their
suite. Teresa was playing games on his tablet as Johnnie
played songs on his keyboard and sang *'Sin is nasty.'*

Karen overheard him and tried to correct him. "Johnnie,
we're in Cincinnati. Can you say that? Cin-cin-na-ti"

Johnnie continued his song of *'Sin is nasty'* in various keys
and increasing and decreasing tempos. Karen decided to let
him continue. She was satisfied that he was trying to
pronounce such a difficult sounding city.

Timothy recently received the contact information for every
performer. He planned to visit them tomorrow during some
of the workshops that were planned. He wanted to pay
special attention to the individuals and groups involved in
the True Psalmist situation.

Timothy continued his research into his prime suspects:
Chosen Cherub. He found one of the few videos of them on
You Tube. He watched it several times and noticed that their
use of lighting effects might be the reason for some of the
hypnotic reactions on some of their audience. He also

noticed that he had difficulty understanding their intentionally slurred lyrics. He was convinced that he had finally found the perfect candidates for the Yahweh's True Psalmist and the Son of Yahweh's True Psalmist. He reasoned that this quartet had the financial resources and wherewithal to pull off the entire Psalmist scam.

'Yes,' he reasoned. *'I can't wait to interview these guys and catch them in a bundle of lies.'* His thoughts were interrupted by the sound of his phone shattering the silence of his self-made sanctuary in the living room of the suite. He started not to respond until he noticed that it was from Zachariah Phillips.

Zachariah's voice appeared to waver indicating he was upset about something. "Brother Timothy, I think we have to eliminate those Chosen Cherub as perhaps our prime suspects."

Timothy was slightly astonished and confused. "Mr. Phillips, I was under the impression that they were probably our prime suspects. What made you change your mind?"

Zachariah added, "I thought we could finally and conclusively have a safe and peaceful convention until these brothers encountered the Psalmist disguised as an old man."

Timothy could not believe what he was hearing. "Are you serious?"

" Yes, I'm extremely serious. In an elaborate plan, the so-called Yahweh's True Psalmist or Son of the Psalmist provided them with a catered meal laced with a laxative. Three of the brothers probably won't be able to attend the meeting that I had planned for all of the concerned parties on tomorrow. Chosen Cherub all threatened to contact the police. I convinced them to hold back, be patient, and that we would handle the situation. I related to them, that with the Lord's help and guidance, we will soon eliminate this caustic nasty threat."

Timothy took a deep breath and had to admit that Little Johnnie was right. They were literally in a place that could and should be considered *Sin Is Nasty*.

Chapter 22

"Setting The Table For A Trap"

"Let their table become a snare before them: and that which should have been for their welfare, let it become a trap."
Psalm 69:22

Teresa was quite upset with her father. "Dad, you promised to take us out for breakfast. Now you tell me you have to go to some dumb old meeting."

Timothy tried to explain. "I can't help it; this is an extremely important meeting."

Karen chimed in, "But Timothy, you promised the kids that you would take them out to the *Pancake Haven* and get them the smiley faced pancakes with whip cream and strawberries."

Timothy apologetically explained, "Listen Karen, this thing is coming to a head soon. Zachariah Phillips has arranged for all parties to meet tomorrow morning in the Cleveland Room. This meeting is very pertinent, not only regarding the other artists, but it is even more relevant to our situation. We've got to settle this harassment and fear that has us all on edge."

Karen suggested, "Why don't we take the kids out for breakfast before the meeting? What time does the meeting start?"

"Hey," Timothy beamed. "That's a great idea. The meeting starts at 9:00, and we could take the kids out to eat about 7:30, and I would be able to get back before the meeting starts. Yeah, that's a great idea."

Karen smiled, "See Timothy, you need someone like me to keep you straight with our children."

Timothy returned the smile, "Yeah, that's right." He was beginning to like the sound of hearing *'our children'*. "I think we need to crash if we're going to get up early on tomorrow." She gave him a quick peck on his cheek and left him to retire on the couch in the living room.

The next morning promptly at 6:30 A.M. sharp, a house keeping woman began camping outside of Timothy's suite. At 7:15 Timothy, Karen, Teresa, and Little Jonnie greeted the woman as they began to exit the room. The woman pushing her cart with various cleaning material remarked, "My, you're leaving mighty early. Would you mind if I cleaned your room now, or should I come back later?"

Timothy held the door open for her and replied, "No problem, Ma'am. We won't be coming back into the room until a little while later. I have a meeting to attend and my family are all going out for breakfast and then to the mall.

167

No problem, just make sure you lock the door when you leave."

The woman nodded, "Yes sir, and I'll make sure to leave some fresh towels for you." The woman craned her neck out the doorway to make sure that they were down the hallway and entering the elevator. She then began to rummage through Timothy's camera equipment. She discovered his notebook tucked between two telephoto zoom lenses. She used her cellphone to photograph items from the notebook that she felt were pertinent. She continued her search in his equipment bag which concluded when she discovered the film canasters that Timothy had placed the OxyContin tablets. She emptied the pills into her pockets, placed the canasters back into their proper place. She then peered sharply both ways down the hall, when she saw that no one was within sight, she hurriedly exited the room with a massive smile on her face. She then climbed up the stairway to the top floor and exited stealthily. She cautiously entered into her room. sat down on her bed, removed her wig, eyelashes, makeup, lipstick, and anything else that might reveal her true sexuality and identity as Yahweh's True Psalmist.

He felt quite content at his masquerade. Using his house-keeping disguise, he was able to persuade one of the actual employees to take over her area. The persuasion was easily accomplished by providing her with some financial motivation. He then began to create what he felt would be the final phase of his Yahweh's True Psalmist mission. He opened his Bible to do research on the next set of items he would provide for his victims.

Karen dropped Timothy off in front of the Convention Center. He rushed to his suite because the meeting was scheduled to begin in five minutes. Timothy grabbed his camera bag, rushed down the corridor, and entered the elevator. The ride to the banquet hall seemed as though it took an eternity as he watched various hotel guests hold up the elevator to allow family members to load their luggage.

When the elevator landed in the main lobby, He found his way to the immense Cleveland Meeting Room. He immediately found a seat and placed his equipment on the floor beneath his chair. He was pleased that he wasn't the last to arrive as he watched the four Ceremonious Dancers find their places opposite him.

There was a look of disapproval on the face of Zachariah Phillips, the Emperor of Gospel Music. He held a large envelope in his hand. "Well, since we're all here, let's get started. Now, I suppose you're wondering what is inside this large, or shall I say humongous envelope."

"Excuse me, Pastor Phillips," Flora-Bea deferentially suggested. "Don't you think we should start with prayer."

Without any sign of discomfort, Zachariah Phillips forced a slight smile of embarrassment on his face, "Yes sister. Why don't you lead us, okay?"

169

The group bowed their heads, and everyone closed their eyes, except for Timothy. He was still coping with his move toward religion. He often wavered in his own belief system.

Flora-Bea began, "Father God, I thank You for this opportunity to praise Your holy Name." Her cousins were steaming internally with envious thoughts but gave a pious outer appearance. She was not aware of anything or anyone in the room except for her concentration on what she felt was her most earnest prayer.

As she continued her prayer Timothy thought he was feeling an aura in the atmosphere. Her voice remained calm and devout. "My Lord, I thought in my prosperity that I would be moved. LORD, by thy favor You have made my mountain to stand strong."

Timothy eased his eyes closed and thought he was feeling a chill running up and down his spine. He tried to keep his thoughts off the prayer so that he would not experience what he felt was *religious hocus-pocus*. *'This whole thing is freaking me out,'* was the thought that constantly circulated in his mind.

He wasn't the only person to experience a chill like feeling creeping up their spines. Flora-Bea resumed, "I cried to You, Oh LORD, and right now we are making this supplication."

Pos-I-Tive Rehema interjected, "Glory. Glory. Glory. He's a wonder in my sanctified soul."

Without missing a beat, Flora-Bea asked God in earnest, "What profit Oh Lord, is there in our blood, when we go down into this pit? This pit of sorry, This pit dug for us by our enemy. This pit of potential death, oh my Lord."

Zachariah Phillips let out of shout of, "Hey. Hey. Yea Lord!"

Flora-Bea pressed on, "If we perish, can our dust praise you? If we perish, how can we declare Your truth? Hear, Oh Lord, and have mercy upon us."

Gabriel echoed her, "Oh Lord, have mercy on me. Have mercy on us."

She resumed, "I believe Lord that You will turn our mourning into dancing." The Ceremonious Dancers tuned into the part about 'dancing'. Her voice intensified, "You have changed my sad clothes and dressed me with gladness."

Timothy managed to pry his eyes open a scant and noticed some type of light glowing around Flora-Bea. He quickly closed his eyes and tried not to focus on the room, the people and especially the prayer.

She raised her hands above her head in surrender and concluded her prayer, "To the end, You are my glory. We sing praises to Thee, and we cannot be silent. Oh LORD, my God, I will give thanks to Thee forever. Amen."

The group mirrored her "Amen". Timothy mumbled, "Oh man, I'm glad this is over." A Bible scholar would have taken note that her prayer was remarkably similar to Psalm 30. Zachariah Phillips summoned every ounce of self-control as he attempted to conceal the anger and disgust that was swelling up within him. He managed to politely respond to Flora-Bea's prayer. "Thank you so much for that inspirational prayer as we commence this meeting. Please forgive me for not taking the initiative to start this gathering with the Lord's blessing."

"That's alright Dad," Amoz remarked as he tried to comfort and assist his father. "We all understand that you're under a great deal of pressure." The group responded with nodded heads of agreement and facial expressions of support.

Zachariah was obviously still distressed but managed to continue. "I'm feeling anguished at this entire situation. I am especially upset today because of what I discovered on this table when I arrived."

Everyone observed that he was holding a large manila envelope in both of his trembling hands. It was quite evident to everyone that the envelope no doubt had something to do with Yahweh's True Psalmist. Zachariah's tenseness and insecurity appeared to be transferred to the entire group. They waited with intense anticipation as Zachariah continued. "I suppose you know this envelope was delivered by that rascal. I'm not even going to repeat his title. I won't give him any credit to Yahweh or any person, or anything that is righteous. I'm sick and tired of this despicable individual."

Pos-I-Tive Rhema decided to provide verbal assistance. "Brother Phillips, on behalf of all of us I would like to extend our sincere and enervating support. May I ask without being haughty or impetuous, could you please give us the details of your discovery of this envelope from this parched up, superficial individual." Some of the group smiled at Pos-I-Tive Rhema's use of his extended vocabulary. To some it brought a sense of relief that everyone in the room was in the self-same situation.

Zachariah Phillips managed to oblige a smile. "When I arrived in this room, I observed that Brother Gabriel from Chosen Cherub was the only person here."

"Woe. Woe. Woe, you can't put this on me! That envelope was on the table when I got here. I never touched it. I noticed that it was addressed to Zachariah Phillips. It was right in the middle of this table."

Myra-Ann from the Ceremonious liturgical dancers rose to her feet focused her attention on Gabriel. "This isn't right. You all stay the farthest from us and you arrive first. " Zachariah motioned for her to take her seat.

"Yeah," Amoz exploded. "Where's the rest of the group? Why aren't they here?" Gabriel attempted to reply, but Amoz ranted on. "My father's car was riddled with bullets

173

not too long ago. My tires were all flattened by this demon. My father has been stressed out since this whole thing began. This is not a plaything. I bet you or your brothers never received any diabolical messages from this so-called Psalmist."

Gabriel cleared his throat. "You can't lay this thing on me. My brothers are all recuperating from an attack from this dude. A catered meal was sent to us laced with some type of laxative. I'm here because I only ate the fruit basket from *Edible Arrangements,* and I didn't touch the other food. I'm seriously thinking about going vegan."

Archduke Joktan Jahnsen, Jr. decided to enter into the fray as accusations were steadily rising against the only Chose Cherub present. "I was attacked and assaulted by this demonic individual. I believe your brothers were no doubt a part of this entire charade." He then increased the volume and vigor of his voice. He focused his eyes directly on Gabriel. "I rebuke you in the Name of Jesus, you are a lying wonder! You certainly weren't chosen by the Lord; more likely, you were chosen by the devil to do his mischief."

Timothy was tempted to retrieve one of his cameras and video the events as they evolved. He decided to just sit still and observe.

Gabriel rose to his feet, shook his fist in defiance and snapped, "How dare you accuse me or my family in this mess. Maybe you don't know this, but we've invested thousands of dollars to make this conference successful. We received contact from this clown late last night. And I declare before you all and my God almighty, that our food was tampered with by someone. We can't say who, but I have a suspicion that it was the work of this diabolical fiend. My brothers are recuperating as we speak. I feel like the servant of Job who declared that he was the only one to survived."

Zachariah did not want the other artists to be aware of the financial support of Chosen Cherub. He realized that he had tried to conceal the support of Chosen Cherub from the others. He had misappropriated most of the funds that were targeted for the convention. He decided that he had to segue away from the financial matter. Zachariah rose to his feet, motioned for calm in the group and suggested, "Let's stop jumping to conclusions, I'll open the envelope and let's see what's inside and see how, and if it will affect us."

Flora-Bea was contemplating praying again but declined when she observed the looks of disapproval on the faces of her cousins. Zachariah Phillips took a deep breath, wiped his brow, closed his eyes, and opened the large envelope with all eyes gazed upon his every movement.

<u>Chapter 23</u>

"Something Fishy Caught

In An Evil Net"

"And As The Fishes That Are Taken In An Evil Net,
And As The Birds That Are Caught In The Snare."
Ecclesiastes 9:12b

The Manila envelope was slowly opened by Zachariah Phillips, the Emperor of Gospel Music. He announced, "There seems to be a sealed envelope for everyone here. I'll distribute them to each of you. Each of you can decide whether or not to reveal its contents. I will leave that choice up to you. I'll distribute them now."

Joktan Jahnsen, Jr., the Archduke received his envelope first. He observed the others waiting for him to open his to determine whether he wanted to reveal the contents.

Archduke Joktan Johnsen, Jr. pronounced that he would divulge the contents to the group. He slowly opened the number 10 envelope. He exhibited a slight smile, and began, "I believe this is from the Psalmist. The heading reads like this: '*Lover and friend hast thou put far from me, and mine acquaintance into darkness. Psalm 88, verse 18.*" He expressed a look of confusion, but he continued reading. '*You have not been faithful to your first love with whom you are married. What you have done in darkness shall come forth in the light. Yahweh's True Psalmist."*

Many in the gathering were assuming that he was accused of not giving his sincere affection toward the church, which should have been his first love. He, however, knew that the reference was not regarding the church being the bride of Christ. He knew that the reference was regarding his unfaithfulness to his wife. He fumed, "This is all nonsense. Everyone knows that I have been faithful to the call of my ministry."

There were no indications from his observers that he was deeply wounded by this message. It was common knowledge that he had been assaulted in the hotel bathtub. However, no one was aware that it was the Psalmist in the person of Lomonsha. He was the only one who knew about his attempted indiscretion with Lomonsha. A tear was welling up in his eyes as he announced. "I've strived all my adult life to uplift the Name of the Lord. This whole message is a monstrosity."

Pos-I-Tive Rhema gently patted him on the back as a sign of encouragement. "We know of your faithfulness. Don't give in to this diabolical antagonistic humbug. You just rest assure that the Omnipotent, Omnipresent Master of this realm is aware of your faithfulness."

Archduke smiled, "Thank you for your support. I really needed those words of encouragement."

Pos-I-Tive Rhema opened his envelope and announced, "Let's see how much more buffoonery this character assassin can emulate upon me." The focal point of the group was now on him. He began reading: *'Thou lovest all devouring words, O thou deceitful tongue. God shall likewise destroy thee for ever, he shall take thee away, and pluck thee out of thy dwelling place, and root thee out of the land of the living. Selah. Psalm 52, verses 4 and 5.' Hear me now, you braggart. The words you flaunt to others as you loot their resources shall bring you destruction. Take heed to the Yahweh's True Psalmist.'*

Timothy knew of Pos-I-Tive Rhema's charitable donations to many needy organizations. Every cent that he received from his role as a Gospel rap artist went to aid the underprivileged. It was obvious that Yahweh's True Psalmist miss the mark regarding the philanthropist Jacob Widbell, better known by his stage name *Pos-I-Tive Rhema.* Timothy felt the need to correct the false information that was rolled out by the Psalmist. However, he had promised Jacob Widbell not to reveal the true facts about his generosity.

The attendees in the group were perplexed by Pos-I-Tive Rhema's reaction. He beamed, "This is pure poppycock. This man is a charlatan. He knows little about our ministries, and I would wager that he knows infinitely less about my walk with the Master. I tell you that this sham artist will be an ignominious failure. In other words, this so-called Yahweh's True Psalmist will suffer great public disgrace and shame."

Myra-Ann, the leader of the Ceremonious liturgical dance troupe volunteered to reveal what was their message. Before opening the letter, she leaned over and whispered to her dance mates, "This Pos-I-Tive Rhema is too much, isn't he? He never talks like that when he performs. I'm a little nervous about what our message might be." She slowly slid the folded paper out and began to read the message. She cleared her throat and began: "Here's our little message from our common foe: *'Let mine adversaries be clothed with shame, and let them cover themselves with their own confusion, as with a mantle. Psalm 106, verse 29. A time to weep, and a time to laugh; a time to mourn, and a time to dance. Ecclesiastes 3, verse 4. Have you any shame, you Jezebels! Repent or suffer my wrath. I, the True Psalmist danced with all my might and was mocked for my sincere holy worship. You shall be mocked by all who cast their eyes upon you for your blasphemous disrespectful roguishness. Yahweh's True Psalmist. Son of Yahweh's True Psalmist.'"*

Pos-I-Tive Rhema assured, "Girls, don't pay any attention to the erroneous tripe displayed in that correspondence."

Florance disagreed strongly with Pos-I-Tive Rhema, "Brother Rhema, I think you need to chill. You didn't notice that our note came from both the Psalmist and his son?"

Myra-Ann interjected, "Girl, I agree with Brother Rhema. This is crazy. We're not paying any attention to this nonsense." The remaining members of the dance group were fully aware of the new erotic-like dance and revealing attire planned for the culminating event. The ladies did not want to suffer any anger retorts from their leader, Myra-Ann. The girls remained tight-lipped. Besides, they could not allow their group to give any credence to the adversary known as Yahweh's True Psalmist and Son of Yahweh's True Psalmist.

Timothy gazed at the bulkiness of one of the two envelopes addressed to him. One of the envelopes had Little Johnnie's name inscribed in bold letters '*In care of Timothy Samuels.*' The sight of the little boy's name brought sheer terror to him. But he was determined to wait and hear more revelations from the other participants. Zachariah Phillips looked at the remaining people who had not revealed the contents of their envelopes and inquired, "Is there anyone else who would like to expose more of this man's craziness?"

Amoz Phillips held his envelope in the air and announced, "I might as well read what mine says." He eased the sheet of paper out of the envelope and began to read. '*To the chief Musician, upon Muthlabben. To the chief Musician for the sons of Korah. I will praise thee, O LORD, with my whole heart; I will shew forth all thy marvelous works. Psalm 1, verse 1. A Song upon Alamoth. God is our refuge and strength, a very present help in trouble. Psalm 46, verse 1.'* Amoz let out a chuckle, "This is totally ridiculous. Why does my note have these words that I've never heard? *Muthlabben* and *Alamoth*, what is that? Brother Rhema, maybe these words are part of your extensive vocabulary."

Pos-I-Tive Rhema utilized his phone to get the definitions of the strange words. He announced, "According to what I have ascertained via Google, *A Song upon Alamoth* means *'A song written for sopranos or for virgins.'* And *Muth Labben* is defined as *'death of Labben* or *the death of the son* or *the death of the fool'*. This sounds like it could very well be a serious threat, Amoz."

Amoz's voice wavered as tears began to swell in his eyes. "Some of you may not take this seriously, but I do. When I was younger, much younger, I was a counter tenor. I could sing extremely high notes. My voice could even compare to a soprano. The fact that this message secretly contained the term 'death' frightens me. This, in my opinion, is a hidden threat aimed at me. I can't forget that my father's car was riddled with bullets. Since he is the Emperor of Gospel Music, his life and perhaps my life, as his son, may also be in danger."

Pos-I-Tive Rhema offered his expressions of regret, "I sincerely ask for your apology if I made light of this egregious situation."

Amoz rose out of his seat, patted Rhema on his back, and declared, "Your apology is accepted. We must all band together and stay prayerful." He watched as Pos-I-Tive Rhema returned to his place and then Amoz slumped down in his seat with his hands concealing his face.

After witnessing Amoz's breakdown, Timothy was becoming more anxious regarding what might be contained in his two envelopes. Particularly the contents of Little Johnnie's envelope. He could not imagine a youngster with autism being targeted. *'Was it because the boy happened to be a musical prodigy?'* He reasoned, *'Maybe there's some jealousy involved.'* He attempted to calm himself as he focused on who would be the next presenter.

Zachariah Phillips felt the urge to bring comfort to his son, Amoz, and divert the attention to his own envelope. "We must continue to remain prayerful," he assured. "Now Amoz, we will all get through this. Let us examine what else we may have to concern ourselves with. I'll open my envelope and read it for all to hear." He warily began to scrutinize the contents, then began his revelation, "Alright, this is what it says. *'He suffered no man to do them wrong: yea, he reproved kings for their sakes. Saying, Touch not mine anointed, and do my prophets no harm. Psalm 105, verses 14 and 15. All the ways of a man are clean in his own eyes; but the LORD weigheth the spirits. Proverbs 16, verse 2' Yahweh's True Psalmist. Son of Yahweh's True Psalmist"* Zachariah perused his audience and then continued. *"How many times must you be reminded that you are no emperor. Yea, an emperor is over kings. I, Yahweh's True Psalmist know your works. And I, Son of Yahweh's True Psalmist am intimately aware of your works. You are a wicked perverted son of Beliah himself. You have abused men, you wicked devil. You have been perverted with your own kinfolk. You have been weighed by my spirit, and you have come up short."*

Everyone's nerves were tightened up more intensely as they observed Zachariah Phillips' face contorted into a look of utter and complete fear. Zachariah's mind was dashing and withering with something that went infinitely beyond fear. He was in panic mode as he reflected, *'Either this man is an agent of the Lord, or an ambassador of Satan himself!'* He made use of every possible way of concealing his authentic reaction. He had to hide his anxiety and trepidation. He concluded that the references of him abusing men and kinfolk was no doubt based on the rumors that have been circulating regarding him. Particularly the gossip about his carnal relationship with his adoptive son, Amoz.

He somehow managed to let out a loud burst of laughter. In his most convincing voice, he declared. "I have never heard of anything so foolish in my entire life. I believe you can rest assure yourselves that this is all a fraud. I tell you; we should not be afraid where there is no fear."

Timothy had a feeling that he hadn't gone deep enough into his walk with Christ to understand the meaning of the term premonition. This feeling or premonition was warning him of the significance of his envelopes. He was tempted to excuse himself, take his envelopes and retreat to the comfort of the couch in his suite. He took mental inventory and decided to remain with the group and deal with any possible consequences. His decision to not excused himself was mooted when Zachariah Phillips announced that they should take a break, get some coffee, use the restroom, or get some fresh air. They would continue the meeting in a half an hour. There were too many eyes trained on the remaining people who had not exposed what was within their envelopes. Timothy gathered his equipment, placed the envelopes in the camera bag and exited the Cleveland Room

Forty-five minutes later everyone returned with anticipation of the next revelation. After several moments of silence, Zachariah Phillips indicated, "Alright, who wants to be next? We need to get this all out in the open now. We do have some workshops, rehearsals, and performances scheduled for later this afternoon."

Hannah of the Celestial Smoley Singers volunteered, "We might as well see what's on our paper, right girls?" Their faces signaled that they were all in agreement. She continued as she opened their envelope. " *'For jealousy is the rage of a man: therefore, he will not spare in the day of vengeance. Proverbs 6, verse 34' I have warned you about your enviousness and covetousness regarding the one that is the Deborah. To the one that is your Lily. Yahweh shall take away your anointing and bestow it upon the Lily-Deborah. Son of Yahweh's True Psalmist.'"* The three Smoley Sisters had a look of dismay and bewilderment on their faces. "If you ask me, Hannah asserted, "This is all a bunch of nonsense." She tore the note up into tiny pieces and flung them in the air and watched them float slowly onto the table.

Nevertheless, Flora-Bea understood the cryptic message. She realized that she had been quite naïve regarding her cousins' behavior. Her family had warned her how treacherous her cousins were. Her mother informed her that she should have realized that she was being used and should be wary of their outer sanctimonious appearances of holiness. Her mother named her 'Flora' because when she was born, she looked like a beautiful flower. Her middle name is 'Bea' and pronounced like 'Bee'. The Biblical name for 'Bee' is Deborah. Flora-Bea analyzed that the reference to Lily-Deborah was in truth a Biblical representation of her own name: Flora-Bea. She wouldn't reveal her revelation and decided to pray and seek the Lord's guidance over the entire situation.

Gabriel from Chosen Cherub waved his envelope in the air to indicate that he was now ready to divulge what was in his tightly sealed envelope. "Wait, let's see what message we have. My brothers and I have been associated with all this mess. I'll read right now so that you'll know we're innocent."

Archduke Joktan interrupted him, "How do we know this is legit? As far as we all know, this is your first contact from the Psalmist. This letter could just be a plant to fool us. Yeah, go ahead and read it. We'll decide if it's the real deal."

Gabriel tore the envelope open and snapped, "Here's what it says. You all act as though I'm guilty or something. Sure, I'll read it. It says, '*And he rode upon a cherub, and did fly, yea, he did fly upon the wings of the wind.' Psalm 18 and verse 10.'* Are you satisfied now?"

Zachariah Phillips asked, "Is that all? No message signed by Yahweh's True Psalmist or Son of Yahweh's True Psalmist? That's all. Just that you are going to fly under the wings?"

Myra-Ann snapped, "Well! Ya'll get a message about flying and what not and we get threats and warnings." Myra-Ann gave him a caustic look and exclaimed, "He's guilty. I tell you; we've got to watch out for him."

Gabriel slammed his hands on the table, leaped to his feet and exited the room. He dialed Raphael's number as he was approaching the main lobby and plopped himself down on the heavily padded chaise lounge chair. Obviously

186

aggravated, he managed to speak in low tones. "Hey Raphael, put this on speaker phone so you all can hear this." He waited a few seconds for the other brothers to confirm that they were listening. "Would you believe that we've been accused of being the instigator of all the attacks on the prime-time artist?"

Jophiel echoed the brothers' feelings. "You must be kidding. After all we did to get this thing off the ground; and this is the thanks we get? We should just pull out and maybe try to get some of our money back."

Michael advised, "No, wait a minute. If we pull out, that will make us look even more guilty than what they think we are. I just got a plan to fix them and prove them wrong."

Michael and his brothers were plotting their plan as the atmosphere in the Cleveland Room was tense enough to slice with a razor. All eyes were now focused on Timothy and his two envelopes. Pos-I-Tive Rhema announced, "Well Brother Samuels, you might as well open your envelopes. Before you do that, would you mind informing us why you have two envelopes?"

Timothy grimaced, "One is addressed to me and the other to my girl's son, Little Johnnie from Philadelphia. "

"Oh," blurted Flora-Bea. "I've heard of him. He's the young prodigy. Please open his first." Inwardly, Flora-Bea was

187

hoping that there wouldn't be any negative arrows thrown at the young child. Everyone in the room felt the urgency for him to start reading the message."

Timothy began, "Alright, here's Little Johnnie's message: *'He shall judge the poor of the people, he shall save the children of the needy, and shall break in pieces the oppressor. Psalm 72, verse 4. Even a child is known by his doings, whether his work be pure, and whether it be right. Proverbs 20, verse 11   Yahweh's True Psalmist. Son of Yahweh's True Psalmist.'* That's all it says."

Timothy let out a sigh of relief until Amoz suggested, "Oh, that actually sounds like Little Johnnie is getting some approval because he is an innocent child."

Zachariah agreed, "Our children are innocent, aren't they? The Scripture does say that perfect praises comes from our children. Now Timothy, it's getting late, let's get this thing over. You are not a performer in any sense of the word, so we can't expect any type of threats regarding you."

Timothy opened the envelope and to his dismay, the Oxycontin pills spilled out of the envelope all over the table. His heart began to race, sweat poured down his forehead, and his throat felt as though it was full of cotton. He mumbled to himself, *'If there is such a thing as a devil, he certainly has found me.'*

"Well Timothy," Zachariah inquired, "Can you explain these pills which I recognize as some type of narcotic?"

Timothy knew that if he tried to explain the truth no one would believe his story had any credence. His mind was confused beyond belief. He decided maybe if he prayed a little, the Lord might give him a way out of this situation. He closed his eyes for a moment and silently urged, *'Jesus, if you are as real as my Aunt Sarah believes, I really, really need your help.'* For some reason, his mind reflected on Perry Mason, Ben Matlock, and Judge Maybelline, and finally Judge Greg Mathis. He vaguely remembered how every court case begins with *'Do you swear to tell the truth, the whole truth, and nothing but the truth. Wow, I can get out of this by telling the truth. Not the whole truth, but just certain parts of the truth.'*

Timothy began his defense. "Mr. Phillips, I can honestly say that I do not know how those bills got into this envelope. I think this unrighteous dude set me up to prevent me from doing the job you assigned to me. I don't know what this is all about. There isn't even a note indicating that this came from this Psalmist dude or dudes. This is a plot to discredit me and my reputation as the photo blogger for G-POW."

Amoz gave him a look of approval and notified his father and the group, "I whole heartedly agree with him, Dad. This looks like a setup to me."

Hannah eyes met his with support and added, "I think the brother is being messed with just like the rest of us. He's not even a performer. Why would he even receive a note from the Psalmist, this brother ain't trying to be a singer, dancer, musician, or even a mime."

Actually, Timothy has a phobia regarding clowns and mimes. Timothy breathed out a sigh of relief as Zachariah smiled broadly and announced, "I concur with both of you. We should ignore these threats and innuendos. I think we should all prepare for our rehearsals and workshops. Let's just stay prayerful regarding this situation and adjourn this meeting. God bless and let's stay steadfast and unmovable."

Chapter 24

"Perform Smoothly Without The Butter"

"The Words Of His Mouth Were Smoother Than Butter,
But War was In His Heart, His Words Were Softer Than Oil,
Yet Were They Drawn Swords."
Psalm 55:21

Zachariah Phillips took a long buff from his cigarette and released the smoke unhurriedly into the air. He was making an effort to relax himself. He placed the cigarette in the ash tray and coughed loudly. '*I have to quit smoking these things,"* he thought. He reasoned his episode of coughing had resumed. Lately, he found that even the slightest encounter with his smoking habit brought on incessive coughing and sometimes gagging. He switched to a so-called all-natural cigarette brand. He felt the menthol in his Marlboros were causing an allergic reaction. His strength and energy were depleted from monitoring the rehearsals and workshops scheduled for the day. He was pleased that nothing unseemly had occurred so far. He assigned his son, Amoz , to make all arrangements for tomorrow's performers. Zachariah felt that by keeping him busy, it would allow him to not stress over the Psalmist. Amoz reluctantly went about checking the sound system, lighting, stage props, musical instruments, and other requirements. When he finally completed his task, he was anxious to return to his penthouse and get some well needed rest.

Timothy Samuels managed to pop in and out of the workshops but was limited in observing certain rehearsals. He lingered longer at the rehearsal for the youth choir accompanied with enthusiasm by Johnnie. Everyone, especially Johnnie, Karen, and Teresa were excited about the final performance scheduled for tomorrow night.

When he eventually returned to his suite, he was flooded with questions from Karen and his daughter. Teresa embraced her dad and cross-examined. "Dad, how did the meeting go? Did you find out who the Psalmist is? How many workshops did you go to?"

Karen interceded, "Woe girl, give him time to breathe."

Teresa continued, "Okay, Karen. Dad can we go back to that pancake place again? Can we?"

Little Johnnie joined in the request. "Pancake place. Pancake place. Please."

Karen decided to assist Timothy. "You kids go into the master bedroom and watch television, play on your tablets, or Johnnie, you can play your keyboard." Teresa took Little Johnnie by the hand and led him out of the room.

Timothy was getting his thoughts together to reveal that Johnnie had received correspondence from the Psalmist. "Karen, I don't want to alarm you or anything, but everyone at the meeting received a note from Yahweh's True Psalmist. Even Little Johnnie." Karen's visage displayed concern as Timothy took her by the hand and explained. "Johnnie's note was perhaps the only note that didn't appear to be threatening. It merely mentioned about the innocence of children, and something about kids having perfect praise."

Karen reassured Timothy, "I agree with you. I don't see how anybody could hurt my baby, but I won't let him out of my sight for a moment."

"I agree."

"Did you receive a note or anything?"

Timothy had to be somewhat court-room honest with her and tell her a partial truth. "I did not receive any written messages from him; however, I think someone went into my camera equipment while we were having breakfast."

"You know Tim, I noticed that the room hadn't been cleaned by that cleaning lady. We didn't even get the clean towels she promised."

"Baby, I hate to admit it, but I think we've been hood-winked by the Psalmist. The cleaning lady no doubt was a phony. Let's make sure that we double lock this room at all times." He subsequently went into more details about what happened during the meeting. Especially the episode regarding Amoz Phillips and Chosen Cherub.

Though they wouldn't acknowledge it, several of the performers debated regarding modifying their presentations for tomorrow's grand finale. The most vocal disagreements occurred between the Ceremonious liturgical dancers. The founder, choreographer, and lead dancer, Myra-Ann insisted that they not change the dance routine or revealing attire. The three other dancers were adamant that the attire and dance movements were too worldly and very inappropriate in a religious setting.

Karoln, was especially upset and even suggested, "Yahweh's True Psalmist's mentioned something about us being clothed with shame and called us Jezebels."

Myra-Ann strongly disagreed, "We shouldn't pay any attention to people who are judging us. Look at all the people we reach through our creativity."

Hazela countered, "Are we at this convention to be creative or to worship?"

Florance added, "We can be creative and worship the Lord without being inappropriate. We could tweak one of our other original movements and eliminate the twerking. And above all, wear some jeans, or perhaps one of our practice outfits."

Myra-Ann was fuming, "Are you kidding me? You wear what to you want, but I'm wearing the newest outfit. You do understand that ballerinas wear the same thing that we're going to wear."

Florance objected firmly, "This is not a ballet; and besides that, ballerinas wear costumes which include tights, and tutus, and slippers. This new attire isn't anything like that."

Hazela interceded, "It's like we're just wearing slightly more than underwear. The only thing this dance will do is get a bunch of old men excited and their wives upset. What glory will the Lord get from this? I don't know about the rest of you, but I refuse to be a part of this."

Myra-Ann pounced, "All of ya'll can just get out of here. You wouldn't have anything or be anything without me. I'll go on the stage all by myself. I don't need any of ya'll."

Florance reminded, "Look girls, all our expenses have already been paid, the flyers, and advertisement have been out for months. We could all get sued for breach of contract. Let's just go along with Myra-Ann and let her have her way."

Myra-Ann with a sense of victory announced, "She's right. We will do the dance as practiced and wear the custom-made costumes." However, Florance, Hazela, and Karolyn later contacted each other by conference call and started plotting a plan to circumvent what they felt was Myra-Ann's ill-suited, profane, and definitely unsanctified planned production.

Pos-I-Tive Rhema rewrote his entire performance. He took pride in using the seemingly unbecoming words found in the Bible and incorporate them into his rap. He created a whole new song based on a Psalm. He felt that he could counter Yahweh's True Psalmist's attacks by using a Psalm as his weapon of defense. He thought, *'I will fight his fire with my own fire. I'll use Psalm 113, verse 7 as a covert message.'* He explained to his wife, "Honey, I found the perfect verse. Listen to this: *'He raiseth up the poor out of the dust, and lifteth the needy out of the dunghill; That he may set him princes, even with the princes of his people.'* You see, I will highlight the word 'dunk' and still get my patented message out."

Gynifer Widbell pointed out, "Yes Jacob, I think that's great. It was shameful how you were wrongly accused by the Psalmist. Do you think you'll have the song completed on time?"

Pos-I-Tive with confidence replied, "With the power of He Who inspires all true worshipers, I will be more than ready for this. For this Mephistophelian imposter shall and will be hung. When I release the power of my creative tongue. And let people know where I'm coming from. And still utilize the Biblical term dung." They both felt even more confident as Pos-I-Tive Rhema continued to generate more rhymes to complete his song repertoire.

Flora-Bea was sent to the restaurant by her three palindrome named cousins to allow them time to conspire against her. Hannah began the discussion, "I really did not understand what our message from the Psalmist meant, but I do know this much. We can't allow her to overshadow us anymore." Arora chimed in, "You're so right, Hannah. Ever since she came into this group, she considered herself to be the star. This isn't Flora-Bea and the Smoley Singers. We are the Celestial Smoley Singers."

Ailia added, "Do you remember when the Supremes changed their name to Diana Ross and the Supremes?"

Hannah chuckled, "And you know David Ruffin tried to change the name of the Temptations to David Ruffin and the Temptations. We'll sing some of our old songs that she never practiced, and she'll just have to try to catch on and look like a fool. She can't lead songs that she doesn't know."

Ailia proposed, "I'll contact our musicians and fill them in on the changes that we've made. This will finally put Flora-Bea in her proper place. To paraphrase the Bible Scripture:

Can anything good come from Newark, New Jersey?" The three cousins doubled over in laughter as Flora-Bea entered the room loaded down with bags of food.

Flora-Bea was oblivious to her cousins' plans. She asked, "What's going on? What's so funny?"

Hannah drawled, "Child, you wouldn't understand. We were just talking about an old *Bowery Boys* movie. You could never understand or depreciate it." The sisters continued their laughter and wouldn't let Hannah in on the banter.

Joktan Johnson, Jr., the Archduke of Gospel music wanted to hook up with another woman, but his wife monitored his movements extremely closely. She had received the following text message and read it to her husband. *"'For there is no faithfulness in their mouth; their inward part is very wickedness; their throat is an open sepulchre; they flatter with their tongue.' Psalm 5, verse 9. You'd better watch and pray. Watch your man because I have been his prey. Yahweh's True Psalmist.'* She immediately asked him for an explanation. "What does this all mean, Baby? Are we being harassed by the same person that bothers the other people?"

Joktan knew precisely what the message meant. He knew full well that it related to his attempted affair with Lomonsha. He grinned widely and insisted, "Baby, I haven't been preying on anyone. He's got it all backwards, he is preying on all of us. The other artists, you, me, and even the little Johnnie kid."

She had heard hearsay regarding her husband's indiscretions, but she steadfastly believed her husband's untruths. "Joktan, I'm not worried about anything that will tear us apart." He kissed her passionately. He was ever so grateful that he could lie so thoroughly and effectively.

Chosen Cherub remained up practically all night rearranging their set for tomorrow. Gabriel proudly announced, "Some time ago I was on You Tube doing some research on Miles Davis, the famous jazz trumpeter."

Raphael teased, "Man, don't go off on one of your exploratory comments and nuggets of wisdom. We have a serious problem and you said that you might have a solution."

Jophiel defended his brother. "Ralph, let him finish. We do have to clear our names."

Gabriel went on. "Look, Herbie Hancock used to be his pianist. Once, Miles who was known for sometimes having unusual and moody behavior on stage, snapped at Herbie, and said, 'Don't play the butter.'"

The three brothers gave him a puzzling look as Michael said, "Brother, you're bird walking as usual. Explain what this means; we don't have all night."

Gabriel resumed, "Listen guys. Herbie Hancock did not understand what Miles meant. He thought about the phrase: *'Don't play the butter'*. He eventually understood what Miles meant was not to add extra notes to his chords. Don't play more than you have to. We've been adding too much butter to our Gospel music. We have too many unnecessary notes, movements, runs, lights, and so on."

Michael gave an expression as though a lightbulb went off in his head. "I think I've got it. Our whole set is too confusing trying to shock people. We've got to make our message and especially our praise simple and to the point. Let's stop slurring our words to confuse people."

Raphael added, "And we still have to remain ourselves. We must remain who we are and still manage to get our message out without confusing our core audience."

Jophiel recalled, "Do you remember when we merged the lyrics to 'Lord, I Love You' to 'Lord, I'm Above You' to 'Lord, I Shove You' to 'Lord I'm Above You'? It was hilarious. Yet, you're right. We have to remove the butter from our music. If we're not careful, we'll slide right into the demonic side."

Raphael cut in, "Yeah, the people were so entranced with the beat and the music until they didn't even notice what our message was."

"Well," Gabriel gloated. "We'll do the opposite. We'll make sure every word, and every syllable is clearly heard and understood. We don't have time to play the game anymore. Playing games with our audience is over. Actually, we weren't playing games with our audience."

Raphael chimed in, "We were playing games with God. We can also change our style of music, can't we? Instead of modifying lower and lower keys of D, we'll modify higher. Instead of modifying lower and lower keys of D, we'll modify higher to other keys."

Michael echoed, "We'll modify higher and then we'll stop changing positions on our keyboards. We'll stay stationary and concentrate on getting our message out. It's strange what Yahweh's True Psalmist meant to harm us, literally helped us. We can premiere our newest harmonious chant: *'God Sure Is Great...Never Been Late...Won't Hes-i-tate...He Has No Hate...Let's Cel-e-brate...God's Sure Is Great'"*

The Chosen Cherub brothers responded in four-part harmony: "Let's Cel-e-brate!"

Chapter 25

"Fear Comes The Judge"

"The LORD shall judge the people: judge me, O LORD, according to my righteousness, and according to mine integrity that is in me."
Psalm 7:8

Zachariah Phillips circulated the following flyer to hype up publicity for the already sold out performance:

Timothy grabbed his camera equipment and urged the others. "Hey, let's go. We're going to be late. I have to check the lighting for proper exposures for stage and audience images."

Karen and the children rushed into the living room. Johnnie was the most excited as he exclaimed, "Yes, hurry. I will play organ tonight."

Karen patted him gently on his head as she beamed, "We're ready Tim, let's go." Teresa was also thrilled because she was part of the National Youth Choir. She was hoping to sing a solo but was quite satisfied that Johnnie was among the young musicians in the band.

Timothy was filled with pride and anticipation of the children's upcoming performance. However, he was still a little apprehensive regarding Yahweh's True Psalmist. It seemed as though the Psalmist had somehow vanished entirely from the scene. Many of the participants had a suspicion that he would wreak havoc on this finale of the convention. Timothy put these thoughts behind him and began to focus on the task at hand.

Timothy utilized the flyer to plan how to capture the highlights of the performances. He took note of the first performers:

Zachariah Phillips and The G-POW Mass Choir

The Emperor of Gospel Music directed the Mass Choir with his usual mastery and control. The musicians and the choir's notes were under the strict guidance of Zachariah Phillips. He was a ruthless disciplinarian during rehearsals. No one wanted to suffer the fury and embarrassment of his wrath. He was known to throw tantrums and toxic insults at anyone, including and especially his son Amoz, when they did not adhere to his harsh and stern directions. This severe discipline resulted in a flawless set of his most well-known songs. The execution of these songs was well received. Their performance concluded with his son Amoz's solo performance of *'Let's Just Praise His Name'*. Most of the audience did not notice that the repeating refrain was primarily based on Prince's *Little Red Corvette*. Prior to the closing vamp, Wilson Paulie's saxophone solo brought the audience to their feet. The ramp was highjacked from Prince's *Raspberry Beret*. The Mass Choir was singing, *'I love the Lord, He's Been good to me all of the time.'* However, a few from the audience including Timothy recognized the tune and began singing, *'Raspberry beret. The kind you find in a second- hand store.'* Timothy already had a warped sense of understanding Gospel music. Zachariah Phillips, the Mass Choir, and Amoz's solo had little if any positive impact on Timothy. Except, of course his usage of Prince's music.

Yahweh's True Psalmist was quite satisfied with the Mass Choir's performance except for the concluding selection. His rage was centered on Zachariah for his use of secular music for a spiritual purpose. He was plotting to ultimately end Zachariah's reign as the Emperor of Gospel Music.

Timothy went back stage to check on Karen and the children as the stage roadies prepared for:

Joktan Jahnson, Jr., The Archduke of Gospel Music
He began his set by trying to explain that he would try to perform in spite of the fact that his throat had been sore for the past few days. Timothy almost dropped his cameras when he heard him trying to lower the expectations of the audience. Timothy was fully aware that there was absolutely nothing wrong with the man's throat that would hinder his performance. Yahweh's True Psalmist's anger was also peaked upon hearing this lame excuse. *'How long must I tolerate this liar? He is not only unfaithful to his wife, but his lies also make him unfaithful to Yahweh. For Yahweh*

declares that a liar shall not tarry in His sight.' The True Psalmist began to plan a method of the Archduke's imminent demise.

Joktan's first note was pitch perfect and strong enough for the engineer to lower the volume of his microphone. An Elderly Lady whispered to her neighbor, "My Lord, if he can hit these notes with a sore throat, I can't wait to hear him sing when the Lord heals him."

Her neighbor tapped her on her shoulder and replied, "Girl, there is nothing wrong with his voice. My pastor's wife says this every time she sings. He just says this to get our sympathy."

The Elderly Lady continued, "You may be right, but the brother can sing."

The neighbor confirmed, "Yes, he can sing, and he ain't bad looking either."

Timothy took note that his songs were executed well but did not go over as well as the Mass Choir's performance.
When the Archduke completed his presentation and display of his vocal talents, he left the stage feeling somewhat disappointed that he was outdone by his rival, Zachariah Phillips.

Timothy's apprehension regarding the Psalmist had decreased as he noticed that nothing threatening had occurred so far. He loaded his cameras with fresh Scandisks to record the performance of the children separately from the other performers. He and Karen were both somewhat nervous about their children performing. However, as soon as Little Johnnie pulled out the stops of both manuals of the Hammond B3 organ, and played the introduction, the two parents totally relaxed. Their relaxation was mixed somehow with the two of them being overly excited. The entire audience, the participants backstage, and even the engineers were transferred out of their environments.

When the children began to sing with Little Johnnie availing himself of the totality of the ability of the organ, the Spirit of the Lord seemed to fill the temple. Yahweh's True Psalmist couldn't phantom any form or type or thought of criticism to place upon the children. Timothy was beyond proud of the children. He actually had to admit that Karen, Teresa, Johnnie, and himself were a family. Yet, he couldn't admit that he was feeling the same Spirit that enveloped everyone. He just couldn't give in to what he felt was a type of mass hypnosis. He almost felt a tear form in his eyes. He thought that admitting that he had a family was close enough in regard to his religious conversion. He would plan to marry Karen one day and follow her Scriptural basis for marriage: *'It is better to marry than to burn'.*

Karen suggested to Timothy after the children's performance that they go somewhere and feed the children. Timothy was well aware that she did not want him to see the next performers. An intermission was scheduled after Ceremonious' performance, but she still insisted that they leave early. Timothy suggested that he would just take a few photos of the beginning of their dance and then they could order something from the Convention Center's cafeteria. Timothy took a few photos of the beginning danced of

The Ceremonious Liturgical Dancers.

Their dance always began with their choreographer and leader, Myra-Ann entering from stage right, and the others enter together from stage left. The photos that Timothy took were only of Myra-Ann's entrance with her scanty dancewear. Karen positioned herself so that Timothy would be aware of her presence and gave him an eye to indicate it was time to exit and feed the kids. He handed her a hand signal indicating to meet him in the foyer.

If Myra-Ann wanted to gain attention, she succeeded, especially with the male audience. The women spectators were not impressed and were somewhat embarrassed. One lady remarked, "Now, this is plain scandalous. What is this world coming to?" She pinched her husband on his shoulder and warned, "You better keep both your eyes on the ceiling or planted on the floor."

Even Zachariah Phillips was somewhat taken back until the three other dancers entered clothed in sleeveless overdress dancewear. From the corner of her eye, Myra-Ann displayed a look of disgust at the disobedience of her fellow dancers. She was even more upset because she thought they had upstaged her. Nonetheless, she and the ladies continued the dance as planned. As Myra-Ann prepared to put her hands on her knees to do the twerking like moves they rehearsed, the ladies surrounded her with hands outstretched and blocked the onlookers' view. In disgust, Myra-Ann exited the stage waving her hands as water flowed from her eyes. Hazela, Karoln, and Florance completed the dance and exited the stage. To Ceremonious amazement, the entire audience leaped to their feet and applauded.

Zachariah Phillips proceeded to the stage with a wireless microphone and proclaimed, "I think Ceremonious outdid themselves today. It was a great interpretation of being covered of our sins by the Holy Trinity."

As Myra-Ann prepared to give her group a tongue lashing, she overheard Zachariah's words of praise and the rousing applause. Hazela, Karoln, and Florance were prepared to be eliminated from the group, Myra-Ann boasted. "I told you that this dance would be a huge success. You girls would be nothing without me." The four girls were shocked at her remarks. Myra-Ann embraced each of them and broke out into sheepish giggling. Hazela, Karoln, and Florance realized that Myra-Ann was taking full credit for the success of their planned sabotage. Ceremonious joined together in congratulatory laughter.

Yahweh's True Psalmist's had an entirely different interpretation regarding their creation. His anger was increasing exponentially as he reasoned. *'This was not a holy dance; it was an affront to Yahweh. This goes beyond the whorish display of the beginning of the dance by Myra-Ann. The three nincompoop dancers were only attempting to coverup the apparent nakedness of their disrespectful leader. This borders on blasphemy from the entire group. For the Word says, 'Praise Him with the dance'. This was no liturgical dance; this was no public worship. Ceremonious will also suffer retribution from Yahweh's True Psalmist.'*

When Timothy and the family returned to the concert hall, the place was buzzing with remarks regarding the groundbreaking performance of Ceremonious. Timothy regretted missing it in its entirety. He contacted a few other photographers who arranged to send him some images that they captured. There was a brief intermission, and the audience exited the concert hall. Yahweh's True Psalmist quickly made his way to his room. Consulted his Bible to verify that his interpretation of Psalm 118, verse 8 was true and accurate. He read the verse repeatedly. *'It is better to trust in the LORD than to put confidence in man.'* He then pulled the following crinkled paper from his Gucci wallet: S&W M&P SHIELD 2.0 9MM PISTOL WITH NO SAFETY, BLACK – 11808.

He paid particular attention to **11808** which indicated to him that his purchase of the  was God ordained. Psalm **118**, verse **08** was the only confirmation he needed to finally execute the will of Yahweh through his True Psalmist. He concealed the small weapon and extra rounds into his suit jacket pockets and headed back toward the concert hall.

Chapter 26
"Yahweh's Truest Psalmists"

"For They Intended Evil Against Thee; They Imagined A Mischievous Device, Which They Are Not Able To Perform." Psalm 21:11

Yahweh's True Psalmist stood unnoticed in the back of the huge auditorium awaiting the performance of **Pos-I-Tive Rhema, Gospel Rap Artist**. The rap artist began his set with some of his well-known spoken selections which included his use of obscure Biblical terms taken from the King James Version of the Scriptures. His fans were delighted to hear his classics, while others tolerated the loud music and boisterous responses from the younger devotees. His last song was well received by everyone, except of course for the Psalmist who detested every syllable he uttered. Timothy had to admit that he liked the musical accompaniment and the flow of rhymes coming from the artist's latest creation, 'Dung':

> *He brought me from the dung*
> *Gave me a song that I have sung*
> *I'm grateful for what He has done*
> *Put praises deep down in my tongue*
> *When Satan had me hung*
> *God raised me rung by rung*
> *I have and will always overcome*
> *He brought me from the dung*

Pos-I-Tive was pleased with his reception from the crowd as his wife gave him a wide smile and a look of approval from the sidelines of the stage.

Yahweh's True Psalmist patted his weapon of destruction gently and thought, *'You may have fooled everyone about your little ditty about the dung. But judgement will come from this gun and bury you in the dung.'*

Timothy was dog-tired as he prepared to cover the final two artists' displays of talent. The Gospel quartet who are under suspicion of being the dreadful Psalmist entered the stage, set up their equipment as Zachariah Phillips presented

Chosen Cherub

The four brothers' musical introduction was longer than expected by everyone, including their hardcore fans. The musicians usually played using minor somber sounding notes, but this selection was surprisingly upbeat. The four brothers did not exchange their positions and remained stationary. Michael clearly vocalized the lyrics in soft spoken tones. Chosen Cherub speaking voices had never been heard during a performance. He then chanted the lyrics as his brothers repeated them in tight harmony. The brothers sang clearly and pronounced and enunciated them with precision. The chanting and response were similar to the style of the Baptist deacons they heard as children. The group's song was brief to the point and well received by all.

Timothy took notice that he was beginning to feel a warm feeling as Chosen Cherub song progressed in chromatic steps into higher keys; even going beyond D sharp all the way up to A flat. The flat footedness and nonmovement of the group and sincere praise brought the entire audience to their feet with hands lifted up. Even some of the distrustful G-POW artists took notice of the presence of the Spirit of the Lord and extended their hands in adoration. Many reasoned, *'The Lord could move and motivate angels and even evil spirits to offer Him praise. After all a portion of the Heavenly Chorus of angels revolted and were expelled from Heaven.'* Other people just appreciated the sound of what they determined to be some type of sincere worship.

Yahweh's True Psalmist couldn't find fault in their performance. In fact, he was delighted that their presentation did not exempt them from some of the other main G-POW performers' accusations and mistrust. Some of the people Yahweh True Psalmist contacted thought Chosen Cherub's entire change of musical direction was done to avoid suspicions. However, some were still hard pressed to explain the movement of the Spirit during Chosen Cherub's newest production. The Psalmist relished in the confusion which he determined to be to his advantage.

It appeared that Chosen Cherub should have set the proper atmosphere for the highly anticipated songs of the
Celestial Mosley Sisters From Lexington Kentucky.

The palindrome sisters, Hannah, Ailia, and Arora's plot to defame their cousin Flora-Bea was in full effect. The three sisters had informed Flora-Bea that they were all going to wear their aquamarine gowns. Flora-Bea was fully dressed in the aquamarine gown and was in the bathroom applying makeup. The three sisters quickly changed to their powder blue gowns and called out to their cousin that they were running late and would meet her at the Performance Center. The sisters managed to conceal themselves from their cousin until they were announced to appear on the stage. When Flora-Bea finally met with her cousins on the stage, she was devastated. She felt totally out of place and found it difficult to hide her disappointment by the treatment of her cousins. Hannah had made arrangements with the musicians to play songs that were unfamiliar to her cousin.

To make matters worse for their cousin, they planned to do a medley. The medley would change before Flora-Bea could catch onto the melody and the lyrics. As soon as she got the feel of the song, Hannah would signal the musicians to change the song, and even change the keys. Flora-Bea took notice that her performance was viewed harshly by the audience. Flora-Bea decided to stick it out until the end of the performance. She exited the stage totally humiliated but remembered the advice that her grandmother always gave her: 'Hold your peace, and let the Lord fight your battles.'

Yahweh's True Psalmist definitely wasn't going to hold his peace. He immediately sent the following text message to the finale performers and Timothy Samuels:

> *Happy shall he be, that taketh and dasheth thy **little ones against the stones.** **Psalm 137:9** Yahweh's True Psalmist*

Zachariah Phillips hastily summoned a meeting for all concerned and their families. The gathering was to take place in Rehearsal Room 5 on the second floor.

Karen was extremely upset about the contents of the text message. "Timothy," she shuddered. "I thought all this nonsense was over. How can anyone threaten to bash our little ones against the stones? This is absurd, Timothy. I think it's time to call in the police."

Timothy did not wish to portray his true feelings, "Look, I don't know much about the Scriptures, but I remember Aunt Sarah telling me that '*no weapon that is made to kill you can hurt you*'. So, let's go to the meeting and see what the others think."

Karen pointed out, "Since when did you start misquoting Scriptures. I don't care what the others think. I'm packing and taking the kids out of here."

"Just wait. We'll all pack and leave right after the meeting. In fact, let's pack now." They packed their luggage, place the bags on the floor in the living room, and headed toward Rehearsal Room 5.

When everyone was settled in the large open spaced area, Zachariah Phillips signaled for silence. Timothy, Karen, and Teresa sat near the organ so they could monitor Little Johnnie. The young man immediately started the organ and pulled out the stops on both manuals. Timothy whispered to him, "Johnnie, you can't play now." Johnnie seemed to understand and was satisfied listening to the hum of the Leslie speaker, peering into the vents of the speaker, and watching the speaker's fan whirl in circles.

Zachariah suggested that Pos-I-Tive Rhema lead them in a word of prayer. Pos-I-Tive Rhema knew the power of words and their usage. He meditated for a moment and then he began. "My Lord, troubles are increased around us. The people say that there is no help for us in you." He paused for a few moments and then continued. "But you, O my Lord are a shield for us. We give you all the glory, for You are the lifter of our heads. We're crying unto You. We know that You will hear us from Your holy hill." He paused again, and took notice of the room, and then continued. "When we laid down and slept last night; we woke up, for You sustained us. We will not be afraid of this adversary, nor one thousand adversaries that have set themselves all around us and against us. Arise Oh Lord, Get up and save us. Oh my God

You have already smitten our enemies upon the cheek bones. You have broken the teeth of the ungodly. And we thank in advance in Jesus' Name. Amen."

The entire room including Little Johnnie echoed 'Amen'. Amoz rose to his feet and repeatedly declared, "Amen! Amen! Amen! Amen! Give praise to the Amen. Give Praise for the Amen. Give praise to Yahweh, He is the Amen."

His father looked at his son with amazement and wondered what had gotten into him.

Amoz in an alarmingly loud voice rumbled, "I say amen to this prayer ripped off from Psalm 3. Yeah, Brother Rhema, you have just paraphrased the words of one of the Original Psalmist. How dare you steal the words of David, one of Yahweh's greatest psalmist." All eyes were focused on Amoz. "Now," he declared. "Is time for Yahweh's True Psalmist to avenge himself." He eased the small automatic weapon from his pocket and pointed it directly at his father.

Everyone was frozen with terror except for Johnnie who watch the fan in the Leslie spin around and around.

Amoz continued with his anger directly toward his father and his vocal directions scattered toward the others. "Nobody move, this is not a toy here. It is time for Yahweh's True Psalmist to get retribution on the so-called Emperor of Gospel Music, for his abuse of me. For the abusive use of his so-called Gospel music. And most importantly, his abuse of the Lord's true ministry of all true psalmists."

Joktan tried to intercede. He approached Amoz, "Listen Amoz, you don't have to go there. Put the gun down and let's talk this thing over."

Amoz let out a fiendish grin and pointed the weapon toward Joktan. "My wrath will be upon you too. Do you remember Lomosha, oh Archduke of Gospel Music? Well, do you?"

Joktan decided to remain silent. The revelation regarding his attempted tryst with Lomonsha was far worse than getting killed.

Raphael from the Chosen Cherub softly spoke to the Ceremonious Dancers who were within earshot. "I told ya'll we weren't a part of this Psalmist mess." The girls were too terrified to respond though they knew he was right.

Amoz exclaimed, "I have enough ammo for every one of you. But the judgement will only be carried out onto the ones that are not true worshippers. To the ones who are not true psalmists. My judgement is toward the jealous ones. The ones who exploit their bodies. The ones who care more about mammon than they do for the Lord's ministry. The ones who lives are wickedly, and yet proclaim the salvation of the One called Jesus the Christ. The One called Yeshua the Messiah."

Timothy placed himself in front of Karen, Teressa, and Little Johnnie to shield his body to protect them.

Without saying a word, Flora-Bea lifted her hands high in the air as if she were surrendering to a Higher Authority. Amoz spoke to set her at ease, "You are in no danger. I know that you are a true worshiper. You are one of Yahweh's True Psalmist. You may put your hands down."

Flora-Bea continued walking slowly towards him and confided, "I'm not surrendering to you, I'm surrendering to my Lord and Savior. So, I'm not afraid if you kill me. I know that if I perish, I perish, but I shall see the King. I'm ready to be with Jesus, are you, Brother Amoz?"

Hannah warned her cousin, "Girl, you better sit down. He ain't playing. I don't think he's wrapped too tight."

Flora-Bea ignored her cousin's request and asked her, "Are you ready to meet Jesus? I won't judge you Hannah, and the rest of ya'll, but I will say, all of us better be ready when He comes."

Timothy knew that he wasn't ready to meet Jesus, or anyone, or anything associated remotely with death. In fact, most of the assembly felt that they weren't ready to meet their Maker.

Flora-Bea stopped and let out a soulful note, "Oh", in the key of A flat."

Little Johnnie played an A flat major chord on the organ. Karen tried to convince the boy to stop playing as Flora-Bea began singing, "Oh sweet wonder. Oh, sweet wonder. Jesus the Son of God. Oh, sweet wonder, Oh sweet wonder, Jesus, the Son of God. " She continued another refrain. "He's a wonder in my soul. He's a wonder in my soul. He's a wonder in my soul. I'm gonna' bless His Name."

Karen then tried to remove Johnnie's hands from the organ, but Amoz interceded. "Leave the child alone. Don't you know that out of the mouths of our children come perfect praise."

Flora-Bea continued singing, "Oh how I love Him. Oh, how I love him. Jesus the Son of God."

Timothy and Karen began to feel at ease as Flora-Bea transitioned the praise to "My soul loves Jesus. My soul loves Jesus. My soul loves Jesus. Bless His Name." Timothy heard this song numerous times at his Uncle's church and he felt the urge to join in singing while lifting his hands. Eventually, the entire group was following the lead of Flora-Bea.

Timothy saw or either imagine a glow or what he was often told was Shekinah Glory surrounding Flora-Bea and Little

Johnnie. He felt a little creepy, but he was convinced that there must be something about singing the songs of praise.

Flora-Bea slowly eased nearer to Amoz and began another praise. "My soul says 'Yes. Yes' Yes' Yes, Lord, Yes, Lord. Yes, Lord. "Eventually she was was close enough to touch him softly on his shoulder. "Son," Zachariah pleaded. "Give her the gun, please. You don't want to hurt anyone, now do you?"

"Can I be blunt, dear father?" Amoz queried sarcastically. His father nodded. Amoz continued, "Shut-up, Emperor. Just shut up. Shut-up, Pastor. Shut-up to everyone of your phony titles. If anyone deserves to die, it's you. It's you, child abuser. It's you, melody thief. You've been abusing me and most of the others under the sound of my voice. You deserve the ultimate punishment from Yahweh's True Psalmist."

Hannah managed to ask, "Why don't you just let us go, and you and your dad can work things out. What did we do for you to want to punish us?"

Hannah's sister, Arora offered her support, "Yeah, that's right. We have been laboring on the battlefield of the Lord for most of our lives."

Amoz waved the weapon in her direction, "You and your sisters are more like battleaxes than someone on the battlefield."

"Who are you to judge us?" Hannah retorted. "We have been faithful to sing praises to the Lord."

Amoz pointed out, "Have you been faithful to your own family? You can't be faithful to a God that you can't see and yet be unfaithful to your cousin who you see and misuse every day. You jealous wicked hypocrites. I, or should I say everyone here noticed that you tried to embarrass and shame her during your dreadful display of covetousness. If the Holy Ghost doesn't hold me back, you sisters should be the first ones that I bust a cap in."

" That's a lie!" Ailia interjected. "That is a bold face lie. We did no such thing. She didn't rehearse these songs. That's why she looked so out of place on that stage. Anyone can see that we love our cousin."

Amoz carefully perused the room and retorted, "Look around you. If blind Bartimaeus were here, he could see through your deception even before he was healed by Jesus. We all know you're lying. Liars all of you Smoley Sisters. Flora-Bea loved you and the rest of us enough to risk her life to save others. If that's not Christ-like, and then you tell me what it is? " The Smoley Sisters had nothing more to say as looks of embarrassments was plastered all over their faces."

Flora-Bea continued singing until she managed to ease closer to Amoz. "Won't you give me the gun, Amoz?" He shook his head and gripped the gun tighter.

Timothy raised his hand as though he was in a classroom and asked, "Amoz, may I speak for myself and my family?" Amoz offered a look of approval. "Look, I've been following you guys for weeks and I'd like to point out a few things, Okay?" Karen hunched him and put her finger up to her lips as a signal to silence him. Timothy continued, "I'll give you a breakdown of what I understood about the effects of your warnings, harassments, and threats. You have even physically hurt some of us."

The group bobbed their heads in agreement, except for Amoz. Timothy said, "This is my school of thought for all of ya'll Gospel singers."

"Go ahead," Amoz said. "I've got to hear this."

Joktan Jahnson, Jr., the Archduke of Gospel Music protested. " I am not called the Archduke of Gospel Music for nothing. I know what I speak about. I know my chosen field. What can you tell us, Mister Photographer? What can you tell us, Mister Blogger? You don't sing, and probably can't hold a tune with glue in your hands. Besides that, you ain't even saved, sanctified, and Holy Ghost field. You may know rhythm and blues, jazz, and even classical music; but brother, you don't know jack about Gospel music."

Karen strongly protested, "He may not know as much as you about this genre of music, but my man definitely knows how to interpret any style of music and how to analyze the people performing. Sometimes, we so-called saved and sanctified people think that we're so Godly until we can't see the worldliness that we portray to others."

Teresa swelled with pride as her fathered resumed. "Let's start with you Amoz. This relationship between you and your father needs to be addressed privately. No offense, but if you genuinely believe in Jesus, then settle this thing between you, your daddy and Jesus. You have to admit, Amoz, that your dad has skills when it comes to bringing out the best during his direction of the Mass Choir. He has also helped so many of the people in this room, and others who performed this week. Give the brother some credit. I suppose we all have our faults. Come on man, work this thing between you and your dad. Ah shucks, it shouldn't have taken you these many years for this to bubble out of you. "

The group gave him light applause but ceased when Amoz gave them looks of disapproval. Timothy knew he was on a roll and pressed on. "Joktan, brother you need to chill with all your drama. You're hiding something from all of us."

Joktan looked over at his wife for some support. "Joktan, your performance was flat. I don't know what ya'll religious call it. Maybe I can just say, brother, if you had a gift or some type of hocus-pocus thing, but you've lost it. Whatever you want to call it, you don't have it anymore. I call your performance not very inspirational. Isn't that what Gospel music is about. To be frank, your whole performance was, shall I say corny."

Joktan was fuming and objected vehemently, "Who made you a music critic?"

Joktan's wife remarks shocked everyone especially Joktan.

"Joktan, I have to admit you were not at your best today. Perhaps the anointing has left you for some reason."

Amoz revealed a slight smirk as he urged, "Brother Timothy, you seem to be doing surprisingly good. I suggest you chill, Joktan."

Michael from Chosen Cherub decided to add some points, "Look, everybody. Amoz was wrong as two left shoes, come on, let's admit it. However, the accusations you all made against me and my brothers encouraged us to focus more on our message. We concentrated on the message, not the performance or our stage presence. We were so used to trying to be different until we lost focus on how to keep our message simply. We removed the butter."

Timothy understood clearly what Michael meant because Miles Davis was one of his favorite Jazz musicians. Timothy smiled and thought, '*I got real respect for these brothers, I suppose they know about Herbie Hancock too.*'

"Yeah," Raphael admitted. "But Amoz, you didn't have to almost kill us with a laxative in order for us to get the message. Who made you judge, jury, and executioner?"

Amoz didn't respond as Timothy continued his remarks. "Mr. Bidwell, A-K-A, also known as Pos-I-Tive Rhema. Your performance was right on the mark without your use of your extensive vocabulary or misuse of those seemingly weird Bible words. There's a great deal lot more that I can say about your ministry, but I'm keeping my promise to you. My Aunt Sarah used to tell that what is done in the dark with be revealed in the light. That goes for the good things as well as the bad things. Now Amoz or Yahweh's True Psalmist or Son of Yahweh's True Psalmist I'm done. Me and my family are leaving. I'm not ready to meet Jesus or whoever my maker is, but we're leaving now."

"If you value lives," Amoz warned. "You and your ready-made family would be wise to remain here. I will let you know when you may leave."

Flora-Bea continued singing in ever an increasing volume as Johnnie continued to follow along with her on the organ. She eased within a few inches of Amoz and then began a new song. "*I will make the darkness light before thee. What is wrong I'll make it right before thee. All your battles I will fight before thee. And the high place I'll bring down.*" There was that glow around her as she continued with the refrain of the famous hymn by Charles Price Jones. "*When thou walkest by the way I'll lead thee, On the fatness of the land I'll feed thee. And a mansion in the sky I'll deed thee, And the high place I'll bring down.*" Everyone took notices that the glow surrounded her and Johnnie as he kept up with every note. The young boy walked over that organ as though several people were playing the same instrument. His little feet could hardly reach the petals as he played octaves and dyads or two notes at a time with amazing skill and dexterity.

Timothy had that feeling of something he didn't quite understand beginning to envelope his body. The Shekinah glory was overwhelming everyone. Flora-Bea's voice managed a high crescendo note as she bellowed "*And the high place. And the high place.*" Somehow, she vocalized a note on the word 'high' that lasted for fifteen seconds and almost shattered the glasses in the room. "And the high places, I'll bring down."

She gently touched Amoz on his shoulder, "Amoz, give me the gun." He slowly handed her the weapon. She embraced him, kiss him gently on his cheek and whispered, "What you meant for evil, God has made good." She then handed the gun to Raphael and announced, "I always trusted you and your brothers." He gave her a broad smile and let out a sigh of relief.

Hannah approached her cousin with a remorseful expression on her face, "Will you ever forgive us?"

Joktan complained, "So, what are we going to do about this so-called, Yahweh's True Psalmist? I say, let's call the police and have him arrested."

"Let's just do what Jesus would do." Pos-I-Tive Rhema suggested. "Those of us who have not sinned, cast the first stone and then in the vernacular, you can call the po-po."

Timothy signaled that he was leaving, waved his hands, and proclaimed, "You religious people figure this out. I'm into music, not salvation."

Zachariah Phillips smiled at Timothy, gave him a thumbs up and rubbed his fingers together to indicate that Timothy could expect a huge bonus for his participation and words of wisdom. The Emperor of Gospel Music had to admit to himself, '*Brother Timothy Samuels may not have the Holy Ghost, but the Lord surely used him today. Praise Jesus.*'

Timothy tapped the young prodigy on his shoulder, motioned for his family to leave. They slowly exited the room, As they made their way to their suite, Timothy announced. "I'm ready for two things, Karen."

Karen asked, "And what are these two things, baby."

Teresa was curious too. "Yeah, Daddy, what are these two things?"

They rushed into the room grabbed the luggage and camera equipment and hustled off to the vehicle. "Well," Timothy continued. "Number one, I don't care why this guy went crazy on us. I don't want to know anything about Yahweh's True Psalmist. Just let the spiritual, religious folks deal with Amoz. We should have known all along that he was the culprit. He probably flattened his own tires and fired at his own father's car. He would be the only one to have everyone's contact information. Number two, I want to get out of 'Sin Is Nasty' as soon as possible. Oh, I lied, there is a third thing."

Karen reminded the children to buckle their seat belts as they entered the vehicle. She reminded Timmy. "Now what is this third thing?"

Timothy guided the car towards the interstate as the two ladies in his life waited patiently for his third thing for which he was ready. "Well?' They petitioned.

Timothy chuckled and soothed their curiousness, "I want a family and I want Karen to always be part of my family."

Teresa asked, "Daddy, what about me and Johnnie being in the family."

Karen clarified Timothy's remarks, "I guess your daddy is trying to propose to me."

Timothy responded, "Well, I guess you can say this is a proposal for all of us."

Karen let out a loud shriek and declared, Timothy, I'll have to think about it."

Teresa yelped, "What?"

Timothy admitted, "It took a lot of me to get this far. Now, I've got to wait while you think about it."

Karen teased, "Ummm, when we get to Philly, you get on your knees, put a ring on my finger and do this the right way."

Teresa leaned back in her seat and supported Karen. "Yeah, Daddy. I'll help you pick out a ring. Johnnie can play the organ and maybe be the ring bearer. I'll be the flower girl. "

Karen said, "Not so fast. I didn't say yes yet."

Timothy took both hands off the steering wheel, raise them in the air and declared, "Help me Lord."

Made in the USA
Middletown, DE
29 January 2021

32316385R00136